Cacti and Succulents

An In-Depth Guide to Maximizing Yield, Quality, and Beauty, Along with the Best Companion Plants for Beginners

Table of Contents

Introduction

Cacti and succulents have been around for generations, but did you know it has been only a few hundred years since humans first began the domestic cultivation of these prickly plants? In the grand scheme of things, cactus farming is still in its infancy. The progress of succulent cultivation has been anything but consistent throughout the ages. It reached a new high on the graph only recently. But that doesn't mean humans don't know much about these thick-leaved plants.

In this book, you will explore everything that humankind has managed to learn about cacti and succulents, what they are, what makes them unique, their scientific names, their uses in ecology and at home, and an explanation of why you should start cultivating these water-retaining delights if you haven't already begun your own garden yet.

Once you are pumped up and ready to begin your journey into the growth of cacti and succulents, you will be introduced to the various species that originated in the Wild West, their natural habitats, and how you can domesticate them. After all, they live in some of the harshest known conditions. Will adapting to the more tolerable atmosphere of your house cause any problems for the plants?

Then, you will dive into the deep recesses of the planting process of cacti and succulents, how they can be grown from different base mediums, their watering cycle, their need for fertilizers, and overall maintenance. Cultivating and maintaining cacti and succulents is much easier than growing and nurturing other types of plants, and you can start reaping the benefits of these thorny plants in no time.

As soon as you have your first succulent fully grown and blooming in all its glory, you will be filled with the urge to cultivate another one. You don't need to follow the same lengthy procedure to develop your second cactus. Later in the book, you will learn the art of propagation and find an in-depth guide to cloning.

By the time you have finished reading, you will not only be able to tackle any challenges you may face post-cultivation but also have a short list of some of the finest companion cacti and succulents at your disposal.

Despite the complicated nature of these bulbous living plants and their biological importance, you will find the information in this book to be accurate and amazingly easy to grasp. It is perfect for beginners, but a seasoned horticulturist will also find a few illuminating facts and techniques here. Get ready to enjoy a wealth of knowledge on cacti and succulents, accompanied by some spectacularly vivid illustrations, which will lead you into this fascinating world.

Chapter 1: The Fascinating World of Cacti and Succulents

Cacti and succulents aren't worlds apart, but they aren't quite the same either. Every cactus is a succulent, but every succulent may not be a cactus. It's like saying every human is an animal, but not all animals are human beings. "Cactus" is the name given to a botanical family, whereas a succulent is a group of plants of which cacti are a part.

You may know what cacti look like. After all, they have been described in various novels and shown in a number of Hollywood movies. They are thorny green bulges that sprout from the ground, devoid of any leaves, typically found in a desert.

Quite bland on the surface, but did you know that they can grow some of the most beautiful flowers? The colors of these flowers are their most remarkable feature. From a brilliant pink to sapphire blue, a sea of full-grown cacti is a vibrant kaleidoscope of scintillating colors that will please even the least artistic eye.

Cacti store water in their thorny spines. These spines act like leaves (they actually aren't), and they perform photosynthesis whenever required. Succulents that are not cacti, on the other hand, usually have leaves that can store water and other nutrients.

That said, there are succulents with spines that aren't cacti. In essence, the absence of leaves is one of the few differentiating features between cacti and succulents.

Cacti are native to the barren lands of the New World, or as it is called today, the Americas. In other parts of the globe, they are domestically cultivated rather than naturally grown. That's because they are some of the easiest plants to nurture.

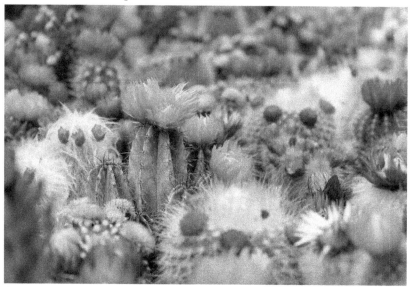

A sea of full-grown cacti is a vibrant kaleidoscope of scintillating colors that will please even the least artistic eye.

https://pixabay.com/photos/cactus-flower-botanical-desert-2721269/

A Brief History of Cacti and Succulents

These days, most people connect cactus with a spiny plant found in arid regions. But the name was originally used in Greek as káktos long before the cactus was discovered in the Americas. Káktos is a spiny sow thistle plant commonly found throughout Europe, northern parts of Africa, and the western regions of Asia. Intrinsically, they are not associated with cactus in any way and have entirely different taxonomies. They only share similar names and spines.

The cactus is a part of the Cactaceae family of plants, a family with an ancient history going back millions of years. However, the cactus you know and love today is relatively new because its fossils haven't yet been found.

Every species of cactus, except the Rhipsalis baccifera, which is found in Africa and Sri Lanka, naturally grows only in the Americas. This fact has given rise to an interesting theory. In an age long past, an era when dinosaurs roamed the Earth, there were no continents, just a single extensive landmass, a supercontinent you could call it. This landmass did not have any cacti, just regular ancient plants, many of which are now extinct.

Then, some 200 million years ago came the breaking up of the world. A huge chunk floated off far to the west, and it was there that first traces of cacti poked and scratched their way to life. This huge chunk is now called the American continent. And since cacti originated after this break, their natural growth does not occur anywhere else in the world.

The modern-day cactus can be traced back to the Aztec civilization (early 15th century), thanks to their clear and accurate drawings. The most prominent pictorial representation (also found on the coat of arms of Mexico) shows a majestic eagle perched atop a classic three-stemmed cactus. When Christopher Columbus discovered America, he carried the first cactus plant to Europe on his return journey.

Succulents, the plants, are so called because of their amazing ability to retain water in their stems and leaves (*sucus* in Latin means "sap"). The reputable Portuguese explorer Vasco da Gama is credited with the discovery of succulents in the southwestern part of Africa. It probably happened around the same time that Columbus discovered America.

Succulents, like cacti, first grew in the semi-arid and arid regions of the world, but unlike cacti, they are naturally found not only in America but also in Africa, Europe, and several areas of Asia.

Since succulents and cacti were present hundreds, and even thousands, of years ago, they were once (in many instances, they still are) an integral part of many cultures.

Cultural Significance

The roots of cactus run deep into the culture of Mexico. After all, the first sightings of the plant in modern civilization were experienced by the Aztecs. As you may know, the Aztec Empire was spread throughout the central part of what is now called Mexico. In fact, the most commonly found species of cactus in Mexico, the nopal cactus, was at the core of the founding of the Aztec civilization. Here's how the story (or myth, depending on your belief) goes.

Aztecs and Mexico

The Aztecs were native to a place called Aztlan, rumored to be somewhere in the southern United States. It was when their god of sun and war, Huitzilopochtli, ordered them to leave Aztlan and find a new home that they set out southward. The god had given them a landmark - see an eagle devouring a serpent atop a prickly pear cactus (nopal) - and that was where they should begin their civilization. They found that landmark in what is now called Mexico City.

Today, apart from being a part of Mexico's national emblem, the cactus also has a significant impact on the culture of its people. Many consider it to be the "plant of life" since it can survive without water for, apparently, several years (in reality, it can survive for a month or two). It is a symbol of hope for many because, after enduring several obstacles, the Aztecs were finally able to find their home.

Native Americans

Mexico's northern counterparts, the Native Americans, also have a high regard for cactus. Their legends go something like this: The cactus was first born after a woman buried herself alive in the ground. It is believed that she rose from the soil as a magnificent cactus with arms stretched toward the heavens. A beautiful circlet of flowers adorned her head every spring, followed by a crop of sumptuous fruit called *bahidaj*.

The Native Americans hold the cactus sacred for its ability to sustain its own life and that of others through its fruit. Its mythology and the beauty of its flowers also bring spiritual comfort to their lives. The Native American affinity for cactus is artistically depicted by the 20th-century painter Ted DeGrazia, in many of his works.

Japanese

Though cacti don't occur naturally in Japan, they are grown throughout the country. The *hanakotoba*, or the art of learning the language of flowers, depicts the flowers of the cactus as a symbol of sexual lust. When a man presents a cactus as a gift to a woman, it implies that he is romantically interested in her.

Chinese

In the Chinese practice of Feng Shui, cacti are considered to bring bad luck. However, if placed on the porch or in the backyard, cacti are believed to repel bad luck from outside, keeping your house free of negative energy.

Succulents

Each succulent has different meanings in many cultures. Aloe Vera was a symbol of beauty for the ancient Egyptians, and it was used to heal wounds during the reign of Alexander the Great. The jade plant is known as the "fortune plant" or "money tree" in various cultures. It is believed to bring positive energy into the house.

Dracaena trifasciata (snake plant) is associated with storms and is generally believed to improve the air quality in its surroundings. Echeveria elegans (Mexican snowball) is native to the northeastern region of Mexico, and it usually symbolizes strength and endurance.

All these incredible cultural and mythological claims about the power of cacti and succulents may have got you wondering whether they are backed up by scientific proof.

Each succulent has different meanings in many cultures.
https://www.pexels.com/photo/assorted-color-flowers-2132227/

Scientific Significance

It was not until Columbus brought the first cactus back to the Old World (15th century) that scientific interest was generated in the plant. Since then, humans have discovered a lot about succulents in general.

Plants usually require quite a bit of moisture to survive. Succulents, on the other hand, can thrive without water for nearly three months. The secret lies in their thick, fleshy stems and leaves. Whenever there is moisture in the soil, they don't drink it all up in one go. They store the excess in their stems and leaves for a rainy day (irony intended), which is why they look so blown up like a balloon.

Visually, you can differentiate cacti from other succulents by the presence of areoles. They are bumps, like acne, on the stem that have spines shooting out of them. Another major part of the plant is the neck, which connects its stem to its roots.

Like other plants, cacti and succulents also undergo photosynthesis, but the process is somewhat reversed. In other plants, transpiration (carbon dioxide absorption) occurs during the day, but in succulents, the process is performed at night. It is done to avoid the loss of moisture stored in their stems.

Succulents are known to have various medicinal uses. Their antiviral and antibacterial properties prevent the occurrence of a number of infections and diseases. Do you tend to urinate more than usual? It could be due to prostate problems, which cacti can help to cure. They are also valuable for keeping your blood sugar levels in check.

Their fruit (if edible) contains vitamin C in abundance, ensuring increased immunity to most diseases. Many of their species are rich in antioxidants, and they also have anti-inflammatory properties.

Furthermore, the different fruits produced by cacti and succulents are generally edible, and the plants are also used as livestock fodder. But these are not the reasons they are popular inclusions in gardening and horticulture.

Entry into Gardening and Horticulture

For generations, humans have been fascinated by the appearance of cacti. From their proven medicinal uses to their probable healing powers, these plants have impacted several sects of people and cultures for centuries. To bring these scientific, spiritual, and visual benefits into their lives, they started looking for ways to bring succulents closer to home.

Since people staying somewhere other than the Americas couldn't gain easy access to the plants, it didn't take them long to figure out how to grow cacti and succulents in their private backyards or greenhouses and, to their delight, it was relatively easy to grow the plants and even easier to nurture them.

An Important Point to Note: While cacti are biologically just succulents, in the world of gardening and horticulture, succulents and cacti are two different entities. When you say that you're cultivating succulents, a fellow gardener will understand that you're growing anything but cacti, but if you're cultivating cacti, you should not say that you're cultivating succulents. Mention cacti specifically.

That said, back in the day, the spines of succulents and their general appearance may have kept many aspiring gardeners and horticulturists disinterested. They weren't grown as often as you would think before the 20th century, though in the last thirty years or so, their popularity has skyrocketed, especially after the advent of social media.

Today, showing off your homegrown succulents has become a trend, and several variants of cactus hashtags are being followed by hundreds of people every day. While there's nothing wrong with following a trend, you need not follow it blindly. Know what you're cultivating before you begin.

Taxonomy and Classification

Succulents are found in over 60 different plant families. The families that primarily contain succulents include Cactaceae, Crassulaceae, Agavoideae, and Aizoaceae. Cactaceae, as you might know by now, is your regular cactus plant with areoles and spines. It includes more than 125 genera and a little over 1600 succulent species. The only species that is naturally found beyond the Americas is the Rhipsalis baccifera. It is regarded to have once been native to the New World, too, but it may have migrated to Africa and Sri Lanka through pollination.

• Crassulaceae

Alternatively called the stonecrop family, Crassulaceae are likely to grow in any arid region of the world. They have succulent leaves that undergo photosynthesis via Crassulacean acid metabolism (CAM), a process similar to that of cacti with nightly transpiration. This family is known to consist of around 1300 species of succulents.

Crassulaceae (stonecrop family) are likely to grow in any arid region of the world.

• Agavoideae

This is a subfamily of the asparagus family of plants. Out of its 600 odd species, 300 are succulents. They are mainly found in the Americas but can grow anywhere in the tropics.

Agavoideae is a subfamily of the asparagus family of plants.

- **Aizoaceae**

This is one of the largest families of succulents, with nearly 2,000 different species. Many of these species are called ice plants since when you look at them under the sun, you can see them shine like ice crystals. Aizoaceae is also called the stone family because, in a land filled with rocks and pebbles, you will be hard-pushed to point out these ice plants.

Aizoaceae is one of the largest families of succulents, with nearly 2,000 different species.
Seweryn Olkowicz, CC BY-SA 2.5 <https://creativecommons.org/licenses/by-sa/2.5>, via Wikimedia Commons: https://commons.wikimedia.org/wiki/File:Aizoaceae_species_Greece.jpg

With thousands of species to consider, it is sometimes hard to differentiate succulents from other plants. You need to keep a lookout for their individual characteristics.

Unique Characteristics

Succulents that are cacti are easy to identify. Does the specimen contain spines and areoles on a bloated stem devoid of leaves? That's definitely a cactus. It is recognizing *other succulents* that sometimes proves difficult!

- **Fleshy Stems**

Touch and squeeze its stem. Is it thick? Does it feel fleshy, like a plump fruit? It's the soft tissue of the succulents that help them efficiently store water.

- **Survival without Water**

Can the plant survive without water for several weeks? Water it once and wait for about seven days. Is it as fresh and healthy as it was on the first day?

- Heat Resistance

Most plants wilt or die in extreme heat. Does your plant seem to thrive in desert-like environments? If so, it is almost sure to be succulent because it probably has spines that are not visible to the naked eye, but they are big enough to keep the plant protected from excessive heat.

- **Thrive in Sandy Soil**

Unlike many other plants, succulents don't need a lot of water. Pot your plant in sand and water it once. Has it survived for a week or two?

Ecological Importance

Succulents don't just look good. They also positively impact the environment around them. Since they grow in a dry, hot climate where no other plants can survive, they are a great source of shelter for the fauna that inhabit the region. Many species of cacti can be given as fodder to domestic livestock, but they may be unpalatable and harmful for human consumption. The fruit of a few succulents is edible, but those of many others aren't recommended to be consumed raw.

The cochineal insect is one of the very few species that has adapted to survive on the water and nutrients of cacti. It feasts on the plant to its heart's content while protecting itself from predators by secreting carminic acid. This acid is used in the production of red dye (primarily used in food coloring and in the production of lipsticks). You won't generally find a single cochineal on a cactus since it reproduces and multiplies into several more while perched on the plant.

Succulents are decent absorbers of carbon dioxide, and since they usually live for more than 100 years, they are an excellent way to combat the growing global warming threat. Admittedly, a tree stores more CO_2 than a cactus, but the latter is easier to grow and care for and takes less space, so you will certainly reduce your carbon footprint with it.

Common Varieties of Cacti and Succulents and Their Benefits

Did you know there are more than 10,000 species of succulents in the world? Of these, there are nearly 1700 species of cacti, from the spiritually revered saguaro to the hallucinogenic peyote.

Succulent species usually differ in shape and form and in the presence or absence of leaves, spines, thorns, and areoles. Their stem may be a perfect sphere or as flat and thick as a pancake. But they all have two things in common, and that's the capability of storing water and their nativity in arid and semi-arid regions.

Not all species of succulents grow without the necessary climatic conditions. The types that are most preferred by gardeners and horticulturists for cultivation are the following:

• **Jade Plant**

The scientific name of the jade plant is Crassula ovata. It is originally from South Africa but is popularly cultivated throughout the globe. From afar, it looks just like a bonsai, but due to its thick leaves, it cannot readily be pruned like one. Its leaves are where it stores water.

The scientific name of the jade plant is Crassula ovata.
https://pixabay.com/photos/jade-succulent-green-plant-5220309/

Many succulent lovers prefer to cultivate this plant in abundance due to the ease with which it can be grown and also because it is low maintenance. It is best known for its healing properties and for curing diarrhea and nausea.

• **Aloe Vera**

Aloe Vera is famous for its skincare benefits, helping you look younger and wrinkle-free regardless of your age. It may reduce the recurrence of any persistent acne as well. The yellow-colored secretion from the plant, called aloe latex, may provide relief from constipation. But don't take it too often, or it may damage your kidneys and even prove fatal.

Aloe Vera is very easy to cultivate and nurture.
https://pixabay.com/photos/aloe-vera-succulent-cactus-botany-678040/

Aloe Vera grows naturally in the northeastern region of Oman and the eastern part of the United Arab Emirates. It can be cultivated anywhere except in places with prolonged snowy winters. It is primarily grown for ornamental purposes since the leaves are long, thick, and green with a jagged border. It is also simple to cultivate and nurture.

• Burro's Tail

Sedum morganianum is its scientific name. It is called burro's (donkey's) tail because its stem dangles from the pot like a donkey's tail. It belongs to the Crassulaceae family, and its natural habitat is in southern Mexico. Due to its unique hanging appearance, its pot is suspended from the ceiling to let its stems dangle freely.

It is called burro's (donkey's) tail because its stem dangles from the pot like a donkey's tail.
https://pixabay.com/photos/burros-tail-succulent-plant-6787172/

Burro's tail doesn't have any scientific or medicinal benefits per se, but any person walking by your house is bound to take a second look at the plant suspended gorgeously on your patio. It is also believed to cleanse your surroundings of negative energy, keeping the door open for positivity.

- **Bunny Ear Cactus**

Scientifically known as Opuntia microdasys, the bunny ear cactus's leaves are shaped like the ears of a bunny or the wings of an angel, depending on your visual preference. Apart from the obvious charming appearance of the plant, the gum secreted from its stem is used to create candles. Additionally, if you boil the stems in water, the soup can be blended with plaster to create a solid wall covering that doesn't chip off with time.

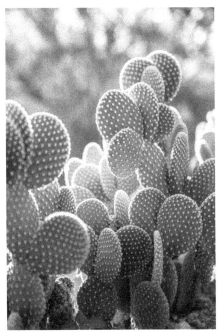

The bunny ear cactus's leaves are shaped like the ears of a bunny or the wings of an angel, depending on your visual preference.
https://unsplash.com/photos/SBKdiLOmylc

The bunny-ear cactus is a natural fog collector, meaning it can catch and store water from fog. It is indigenous to the desert regions of Mexico. A fair warning: the thin, tiny thorns on the cactus's stems can cause prolonged skin itching if touched. It is recommended to remove them soon after they grow.

• Snake Plant

As the name suggests, the snake plant is shaped like a slender, limbless snake. Scientifically called Dracaena trifasciata, it doesn't have any visible stems. Thus, its water storage and photosynthesis all occur in its leaves. It is one of the few succulents that can thrive in a relatively dark environment, making it perfect for potting indoors where there is little sunlight.

The snake plant is shaped like a slender, limbless snake.
https://unsplash.com/photos/iIuyXTcEBTI

For those who want more than just the snake plant's ornamental appeal, sleep in the room where it's placed. You will wake up to the smell of fresh, unadulterated air. Indeed, research has proven that the plant filters the air in its surroundings. Naturally occurring in West Africa, the natives often use it to soothe ear infections.

• Prickly Pear Cactus

The prickly pear cactus, or Opuntia, is among the most commonly cultivated cacti on the planet, thanks to its bright, semi-opaque flowers and delicious fruit. Its stems are often pad-like, similar to the bunny-ear cactus. The early growth of these pads is as beautiful as its flowers. It starts off as a small, pink-colored bud that grows into a large, flat, oval-shaped stem.

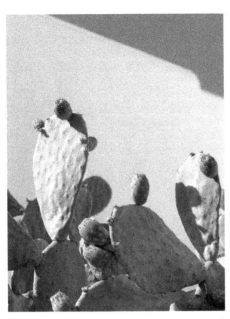

Opuntia, is among the most commonly cultivated cacti on the planet, thanks to its bright, semi-opaque flowers and delicious fruit.

https://unsplash.com/photos/DX_WW_J9Yh8

The prickly pear is native to many regions of the American continent, including Mexico, the United States, and the Caribbean islands. Its fruit is popular throughout its native lands and beyond. If you are eating a cactus fruit, chances are that it comes from the prickly pear.

Its probable medicinal uses include reducing inflammation, healing wounds, and even bringing down the risk of diabetes and obesity. The other well-proven uses of Opuntia are cochineal dye production, animal fodder, a leather alternative, fuel, and bioplastic production. Also, it is one of the easiest outdoor cacti to grow in your backyard.

As you may have noticed, two glaring benefits of cacti and succulents for gardening and horticulture are common to all plants.

1. They are easy to cultivate (among the easiest garden plants, in fact).
2. They are easy to maintain (water is rarely ever required due to their amazing storage capacity).

And you don't even need a lot of space to cultivate most succulents. A regular-sized pot or a small area in your yard is enough to make them grow and enhance your environment, not only visually but spiritually as well.

Chapter 2: Cacti and Succulent Selection: Which Should You Choose?

Now that you have learned about cacti and succulents, you may be wondering which plants are the better options for you. You should consider a few things first, like whether you live in a house with a garden or an apartment with a balcony. You should also consider your goal for the plant, your available resources, and the growing conditions.

This chapter provides you with all the information you need to decide between cacti and succulents.

Things to Consider Before Buying a Cactus or a Succulent

Some people just choose the best-looking cactus or succulent they find and then realize that the plant isn't really a good fit for their home. So, keep these things in mind before you make a purchase:

Garden vs. Balcony

Cacti and succulents can grow either indoors or outdoors. Although they prefer an indoor environment, many types can thrive outdoors. Before buying, check the tag for information. Make sure that the cactus gets enough sunlight every day. Don't place it in a shady area of your garden unless it thrives better in the shade. If you are going to keep it indoors, and it is a variety that likes sunshine, place it on a balcony or on a window ledge and make sure it is exposed to sunlight.

Cacti and succulents can grow either indoors or outdoors.
https://www.pexels.com/photo/clear-glass-table-decor-2100238/

Succulents prefer sunlight, so make sure they get enough every day. Orange, purple, and red succulents need a lot of sun exposure, so place them in the right spot at your home. Bright-colored succulents will be perfect for a house with a garden where they get to be in direct sunlight all day. If you live in an apartment, green succulents can be a good option for you.

Goals for Having a Cactus or Succulent

The second thing you should consider is your goal. Are you buying cacti or succulents for decoration or outdoor landscaping? If it's for decoration, make sure you have the right space for it in your home. However, if it's for creating a landscape, you will need a house with a garden. Since both cacti and succulents are decorative plants, this choice can be made using personal preference, but it is worth considering different plant heights.

If you use the plant for decoration, choose one with a pleasant scent. There are many cacti and succulents with flowery fragrances.

Plant Preference

Cacti and succulents can be prickly, flowery, colorful, or fruity. Before you make a choice, think about what you want. Perhaps a flowery cactus or succulent can be better for indoor decor, while the fruity ones are a better fit for your landscape. Colorful succulents can make a great addition to your garden, while colorful cacti are perfect for both. There is no right or wrong choice. This is about your taste.

Available Resources

Are you ready to add one of these plants to your home? Just like pets, plants are a huge responsibility, and they have needs that you should keep in mind. Make sure to prepare suitable pots for them. Find the right size, material, style, and drainage for your plant. For instance, succulents don't need a lot of water, so choose pots that have drainage holes. You should also prepare the proper position and make sure that your windows, balcony, or garden get enough light so your plants can thrive. This part will be explained in detail in the next chapter.

Growing Conditions

You must make sure you have the right growing conditions for your plant. Although both plants can grow in different climates, some types do better in cold weather than others. You should also consider the humidity level, temperature, and general weather conditions in your area. Choose the cactus or succulent type that is right for your climate.

Types of Cacti

This part will cover different types of cacti, together with giving helpful information so you can choose the right cactus for your environment and needs.

Bunny Ear Cactus

The bunny-ear cactus, also called polka-dot cactus, angel's wings, or bunny cactus, originates from Mexico. It is one of the most popular flowering types. Just like the name suggests, the plant's green parts are pretty similar in shape to a bunny's ears. It is a cute plant that is funny to look at, so it can be a lovely addition to your office and will surely put a smile on your face. It usually grows to about 23 inches, but it can take years to reach this height, as it is a slow-growing cactus.

Indoors vs. Outdoors

The Bunny Ear cactus grows indoors.

Home Decor or Landscape

Sometimes, pretty yellow flowers blossom on the cactus, which makes it a perfect plant to decorate your home.

Sunlight

It requires about eight hours of direct sunlight every day.

Water

Only water the bunny-ear cactus when the soil dries out.

Soil

Dry and well-draining.

Climate

The bunny-ear cactus can't tolerate cold weather and only does well in temperatures between 70 °F and 100 °F.

Old Man of the Mountain Cactus

You are probably wondering where this plant got its interesting name from. Well, it is covered with white and fine hair like an old man, making the name perfect for it. It is also called the Old Man of the Andes, and it originated in South America. At times, the hair can look like wool, giving it a distinctive look. The cactus spines are red and stiff and are easily distinguished against the white hair.

This plant is covered with white and fine hair, like an old man.

Indoors vs. Outdoors

The old man of the mountain cactus is an indoor plant. It is slow-growing and can reach two feet tall, but if it's planted in small pots, its growth will be limited.

Home Decor or Landscape

It is a decorative house plant.

Sunlight

It requires direct sunlight.

Water

Water it every 12 days during the summer and twice a month in the winter.

Soil

Well-draining soil.

Climate

Although it thrives better in heat, the plant can tolerate frost.

Walking Stick Cactus

The walking stick cactus has an interesting and particular appearance. It is a very thin plant, hence the name, and is covered with white, tiny, and sharp spines. The plant is also called the spiny cholla and the cane cholla and can reach a height of 4 feet. It grows a yellow fruit in the summer that you may mistake for a flower.

Indoors vs. Outdoors

The walking stick cactus can grow indoors and outdoors.

Home Decor or Landscape

With its unusual appearance, the walking stick is the ideal decorative plant. Since it can grow outdoors, it is also perfect for your landscape.

Sunlight

Direct sunlight.

Water

Water it every ten days while it's growing and once a month in the winter.

Soil

Well-draining soil.

Climate

The plant thrives in dry weather.

San Pedro Cactus

The San Pedro cactus is a green plant with white and tiny spines. It can grow to a height of 20 feet, and white-scented flowers bloom on its pads at night.

The San Pedro cactus is a green plant with white and tiny spines.

https://www.pexels.com/photo/green-san-pedro-cactus-10109786/

Indoors vs. Outdoors

The San Pedro cactus can grow indoors or outdoors. If you plant it in a small pot, it will limit its growth.

Home Decor or Landscape

With its beautiful, scented flower and eye-catching green color, the San Pedro cactus is a great decorative plant.

Sunlight

This cactus requires direct sunlight to grow and doesn't do well in the shade.

Water

Only water it when the soil is dry.

Soil

Water-permeable soil.

Climate

It can grow in warm temperatures but won't survive the frost.

Brazilian Prickly Pear Cactus

The Brazilian prickly pear cactus is another interesting-looking plant. It has rounded and flat pads with flowers blooming over them. It also has small spines growing all over it and orange and yellow flowers blooming. The flowers transform into orange, purple, and yellow bulbs that resemble a pear, hence the name. The pears are edible and have a wonderful fruity fragrance. The Brazilian prickly pear cactus can reach 30 feet in height.

Indoors vs. Outdoors

The Brazilian prickly pear cactus can grow indoors or outdoors.

Home Decor or Landscape

It can be a decorative houseplant.

Sunlight

This cactus needs direct sunlight, but if you keep it indoors, make sure to place it on the balcony or near a window to get indirect bright light.

Water

Water the cactus when the soil dries out.

Soil

Well-draining soil.

Climate

The plant thrives in the summer and warm climates but can wither in extremely hot weather. It can tolerate the cold weather, provided you keep it dry.

Strawberry Cactus

The strawberry cactus is also called the hedgehog cactus because of its tiny and spiky stems. It is a desert plant with beautiful deep pink spring flowers and can grow up to 3.5 inches.

Indoors vs. Outdoors

The strawberry cactus is an outdoor plant.

Home Decor or Landscape

The strawberry cactus will be perfect for your landscape if you live in a dry environment. The cactus's spines can be gray, white, brown, and yellow, which can make your garden look colorful.

Sunlight

This cactus requires either full or indirect sunlight.

Water

Water it once a month during the winter and twice a month in the summer.

Soil

Well-draining soil.

Climate

Hot, dry climate.

The Old Man Cactus

The old man cactus is covered with thicker hair than the old man of the mountain cactus, and it looks like it is wearing a fur coat. Beneath the thick white hair are tiny, sharp spines. It can reach a height of fifty-two feet and can grow white, yellow, or red flowers, but it can take 10 years for the flowers to bloom.

Indoors vs. Outdoors

The old man cactus can grow indoors and outdoors.

Home Decoration or Landscape

The cactus can be a houseplant, as its wooly appearance makes an interesting decoration. It can also be a great addition to your garden.

Sunlight

It requires direct sunlight but thrives better in light afternoon shade.

Water

Only water it when the soil is dry.

Soil

Well-draining soil.

Climate

The cactus thrives in warm weather and can't tolerate the cold.

The Queen of the Night Cactus

The queen of the night cactus blooms into stunning white flowers once a year, at night, which is how it gets its interesting name. It is also called

Dutchman's pipe cactus. It is native to South America and Southern Mexico. It can grow up to twenty feet tall. Its flowers grow over the cactus's green stems and have a subtle, soft scent. They grow 11 inches long and five inches wide. The flowers' large size gives them a unique feature.

The queen of the night cactus blooms into stunning white flowers once a year, at night, which is how it gets its interesting name.

https://pixabay.com/photos/queen-of-the-night-cactus-flower-7279135/

Indoors vs. Outdoor

The queen of the night cactus thrives in an indoor environment.

Home Decoration or Landscape

Thanks to its beautiful, large flowers, it can be a decorative houseplant.

Sunlight

The plant needs direct sunlight to grow, but only for a few hours in the morning; it then requires indirect light.

Water

Only water the plant when the soil dries.

Soil

Airy and well-drained soil.

Climate

Semi-desert and tropical climates. It can tolerate extremely cold weather for a short amount of time. However, if it is exposed for a prolonged time, it will wither and die.

Old Lady Cactus

The old lady cactus is round and covered with tiny spines. It can reach a height of 20 inches and blossoms into reddish-purple flowers that grow in a circular shape on top of the plant.

Indoors vs. Outdoors

The old lady cactus can grow indoors and outdoors.

Home Decoration or Landscape

It is a decorative plant.

Sunlight

It requires direct sunlight but can also thrive in indirect sunlight.

Water

Water once a month during the winter and every week in the summer.

Soil

Mixed soil.

Climate

The cactus thrives in warm weather but can struggle in extreme heat. Keep it dry in the winter.

Christmas Cactus

Christmas cactus originated in Brazil, and it is one of the most popular indoor plants in the world. It has long, flat stems and no leaves. In the winter, it blossoms into red, yellow, pink, and white flowers.

The Christmas cactus originated in Brazil.
https://pixabay.com/photos/plant-leaf-nature-cactus-3101751/

Indoors vs. Outdoors

The Christmas cactus is an indoor plant.

Home Decoration or Landscape

Thanks to its trailing stems, you can place it on surfaces or hang it from baskets.

Sunlight

It requires indirect sunlight to grow.

Water

Water the cactus every week or two weeks.

Soil

Acidic soil.

Climate

The plant thrives in a humid environment.

Types of Succulents

Now, you will learn about different types of succulents.

Starfish Succulent

The starfish succulent owes its name to its beautiful flower that resembles a starfish. The flower is reddish-purple, deep red, or orange. However, its scent doesn't match its beautiful colors as it smells like rotting meat to attract insects. It can grow to 12 feet tall.

The starfish succulent owes its name to its beautiful flower that resembles a starfish.
Red Bead Dragon, CC BY-SA 4.0 <https://creativecommons.org/licenses/by-sa/4.0>, via Wikimedia Commons:
https://commons.wikimedia.org/wiki/File:Stapelia_Grandiflora_Flower.jpg

Indoors vs. Outdoors

The starfish succulent can grow indoors and outdoors. Since it has an unpleasant odor, it's better if you keep it outdoors.

Home Decoration or Landscape

It can be used as a decorative plant.

Sunlight

It requires full and direct sunlight and can also thrive in bright indirect light.

Water

Water it once a month during summer and spring and every two months in the fall and winter.

Soil

Well-draining soil.

Climate

The starfish succulent thrives in warm weather and can tolerate freezing weather but only for short periods, and the soil must be kept dry.

Afrikaans Succulent

Afrikaans succulents are pretty plants with big and flat leaves. They grow upward and have yellow or white flowers. Interestingly, when the leaves are fully grown, they split out to look like a peace sign.

Indoors vs. Outdoors

Afrikaans succulents can grow indoors.

Home Decoration or Landscape

Afrikaans succulent is a perfect decorative plant.

Sunlight

The plant requires direct sunlight.

Water

Water the succulent when the soil dries out.

Soil

Loose, grainy soil mixture.

Climate

Warm climate.

Aloe Vera Succulent

Aloe Vera is one of the most popular succulents since it is known for its cooling effects. The aloe Vera gel is extracted from the leaves and is used in treating many skin conditions like rashes and sunburns. It is also a pretty plant with a stunning bright green color.

Indoors vs. Outdoors

Aloe Vera can grow indoors and outdoors.

Home Decoration or Landscape

It is a decorative plant.

Sunlight

The plant needs direct sunlight to grow.

Water

Water when the soil dries out.

Soil

Mixed soil with lava rock and perlite.

Climate

It thrives in hot and dry climates and should be kept indoors during the winter.

Jade Succulent

The Jade is another popular succulent since many people use it to decorate their homes. It is a slow-growing plant with a lifespan of 70 years. It can grow up to six feet tall and has woody and thick stems with oval-shaped leaves.

Indoors vs. Outdoors

Jade plants can grow indoors and outdoors.

Home Decoration or Landscape

It can be a houseplant and adds a lovely ambiance to your home.

Sunlight

It requires full and direct sunlight.

Water

Water when the soil dries out.

Soil

Well-drained and acidic soil.

Climate

It thrives in a warm environment and can even survive in the frost.

Mexican Snowball Succulent

The Mexican snowball is also called Mexican gem and white Mexican rose. The plant is known for its silver-green and blue-green leaves that have a rosette shape. It originated in Mexico and usually thrives in a semi-desert environment.

Indoors vs. Outdoors

Mexican snowballs can grow indoors and outdoors.

Home Decor or Landscape

People from all over the world decorate their homes with this succulent.

Sunlight

It requires direct sunlight.

Water

It doesn't need much water, so only water it when the soil dries out.

Soil

It requires well-drained and acidic soil.

Climate

The plant thrives in hot and dry climates but will struggle in humid weather, and it can't tolerate extreme winters.

Crown of Thorns Succulent

The crown of thorns can grow up to six feet tall. However, if you plant it indoors in a small pot, it will limit its growth, and it will only reach two feet in height. It has green and thick leaves, but they are covered in thorns, which is where the name comes from. The plant blooms into producing white, yellow, pink, orange, or red flowers.

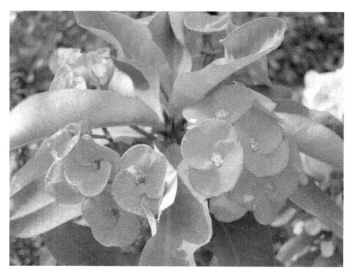

The plant blooms into producing white, yellow, pink, orange, or red flowers.

Indoors vs. Outdoors

It can grow either indoors or outdoors.

Decorative or Landscape

It is one of the most popular decorative houseplants in the world.

Sunlight

It can thrive in full or partial sunlight.

Water

Water when the soil dries out.

Soil

Well-drained and neutral soil.

Climate

Warm and dry weather.

Chocolate Soldier Succulent

Chocolate soldier succulent, also known as the panda plant, is a pretty and attractive plant that you find in many households. It has pale green leaves with brown spots and is covered in white-gray fuzz. It is slow-growing and can reach 2 feet in height.

Indoors vs. Outdoors

Chocolate soldier can thrive outdoors in warm weather but prefer an indoor environment.

Decorative or Landscape

It is an attractive plant that is used to decorate many homes.

Sunlight

The plant will wither in direct sun exposure; it only thrives in indirect sunlight.

Water

Water when the soil dries out.

Soil

Well-draining, neutral, and acidic soil.

Climate

It can't tolerate extremely cold weather and thrives in warm to hot weather.

Flaming Katy Succulent

The plant has green, oval-shaped leaves. Under direct sunlight, some varieties have red leaves. It has small white, salmon, orange, yellow, pink, and red flowers.

Indoors vs. Outdoors

It thrives outdoors during the summer but prefers an indoor environment in the winter.

Decorative or Landscape

The flaming Katy can be an ornamental houseplant.

Sunlight

When planted outdoors, it requires full sun exposure or partial shade, while indoors, it needs indirect light.

Water

Water it every few weeks.

Soil

Sandy, well-drained, acidic, and neutral soil.

Climate

It thrives in warm weather and can't tolerate the cold.

Ponytail Palm Succulent

The ponytail palm succulent is an extremely popular office plant. It can grow up to thirty feet tall outdoors. It can grow to be a large tree, bigger and taller than many homes. When planted indoors, it only reaches six feet tall. It originated in Central America, and it can take years to grow. It has a long lifespan, so it will be with you for a long time.

Indoors vs. Outdoors

It can grow indoors and outdoors. Plant it indoors if you want to restrict its growth.

Sunlight

It requires direct sunlight or indirect sunlight exposure.

Water

Water it every two weeks during the summer and every month in the winter.

Climate

It thrives in warm weather and can tolerate extreme cold for a short period.

Quiz

Now that you have become familiar with different types of cacti and succulents, take this quiz to determine which one is the right fit for you.

1. **Do you live in a warm or cold climate?**
   - Warm climate
   - Cold climate

2. **Do you have a garden in your home for outdoor plants?**
   - Yes
   - No

3. **Do you have a window or balcony for indoor plants that require sunlight?**
   - Yes
   - No

4. **Do you prefer flowering plants or ones that are covered with white hair?**

   - Flowering plants
   - White-haired

5. **Do you think you can provide the appropriate growing conditions for your plant?**

   - Yes
   - No

Now check your answers, then go over the list again and narrow down your options. You are now ready to make the right choice for your needs.

There are many types of cacti and succulents. Some grow indoors, some grow outdoors, while others can thrive in both. Some plants can be a nice decorative addition to your home, while others can be a perfect plant for your garden. There isn't a right or wrong choice. You just need to find a plant that fits your imagination and living space.

Make sure you consider all aspects before making a choice, and don't ignore the plant's scent. Some have an unpleasant odor, while others can be flowery or fruity. Although it is tempting to choose one based on its attractive shape or colors, it may not thrive in your environment. So don't make a rushed decision.

Chapter 3: Planting and Arranging Your Cacti and Succulents

So, you visited your local plant distributor, picked out a beautiful and unusual assortment of cacti and succulents, and took them to their new home. Now what? There are so many variables of gardening techniques to consider for these exquisite plants. Should you plant the succulents and cacti together? Should you plant them separately? Do you use one pot or more? What soil preparations should you consider? How will you arrange them - individually and collectively? This and so many other questions will be addressed and answered throughout this chapter.

To avoid any confusion as you move along, remember all cacti can be considered succulents, but not all succulents are considered to be cacti. They are similar in many ways: they are both resistant to heat and lack of water, and both have thick structures. However, if you explore their differences, cacti are known for the spikes that emerge from the plant's surface that reduce the air flowing around it to optimize the water supply and protect the plant.

Another major difference between them is the photosynthesis technique. With cacti, the process takes place through the stem rather than the leaves, as happens in succulents and other plants. This is why cacti require much less water to survive and are able to withstand harsher environments.

These resilient and undemanding plants can add color and alter your garden landscape into an unforgettable aesthetic. Taking on the challenge of mixing and matching plants can be unnerving. To give you a hand with this daunting task, you'll find a step-by-step guide on what to do and what to avoid as you get further into the chapter.

Indoors vs. Outdoors

Transferring your cacti and succulents indoors is a possibility as long as you are able to replicate the environment they come from. This usually involves an abundance of light, well-drained and dry soil, and cool temperatures inside.

- Placing your plants near a window should ensure light exposure and lower nightly temperatures.
- Some cacti tend to flower and thrive in an indoor environment, though don't be fooled by unscrupulous sellers trying to sell you plants not suited to an indoor environment.
- Among the cacti that flower indoors are Lobivia and Rebutia.
- Lower humidity indoors tends to agree with some of the species; levels that are no lower than 10% and no higher than 30%.

Outdoor succulents tend to grow and prosper in the summer sun.

- As the spring rolls around and the weather becomes hotter, start by moving them into a shady area of your landscape or garden.
- Slowly but surely, start the transition into sunnier locations as the plants adapt to the sun.
- Try to place them in areas where they won't be exposed to the sun's direct heat from around mid-morning to midday and slightly after (from 11 a.m. to 3 p.m.).
- Once you've made the transfer outdoors, cacti may very well not require watering – *but do check them regularly.* As for succulents, they may need a little bit more moisture than the cacti.

Planting Locations

First, start by deciding whether you're planting them individually or together and what is required when choosing the location either way.

Planting Cacti Alone

The best time to plant cacti is in spring and summer. Cacti can be planted inside or outdoors as long as there is enough light for them to thrive. The next issue is the kind of soil. The main thing to consider with the soil you choose is that it should be well-draining.

If you're going to choose to plant them indoors, make sure that they are either facing south or west windows. If you're looking to move your indoor plants to your outside landscape, start by placing them in a protected area at first. Gradually, as they get used to the outside environment, start moving them to areas with more sun.

When considering containers, go for small and shallow ones. Cacti have shallow, slow-growing roots, so they don't need deep containers.

Consider adding small pebbles and rocks to the bottom of your container or an elevated bed. Make sure that the potting mix you use is specifically designed for cacti, as most other mixes may hold more water than needed, which could lead to problems.

The best time to plant cacti is in spring and summer.
https://www.pexels.com/photo/three-potted-cactus-plants-1903965/

Planting Succulents Alone

Succulents are slightly more sensitive than cacti, and that does not diminish their resilience. Make sure you are familiar with the kind of succulents you're planning to grow and whether they are more suitable for indoor or outdoor environments. Some may not withstand extreme conditions like others.

Like cacti, soil drainage is a vital factor when planting succulents. To improve that quality, try adding pumice or sand to your soil. Succulents do not fare well in wet soil, and materials that can help loosen the soil are small gravel, surface, and perlite.

Like cacti, succulents are better suited to smaller and shallower pots. When planting, make sure not to backfill the soil. Allowing for the gaps of air ensures the growth of new roots near the surface, where they are able to breathe.

Make sure you are familiar with the kind of succulents you're planning to grow and whether they are more suitable for indoor or outdoor environments.

Planting Cacti and Succulents Together

If you choose to plant these two plants together, remember that they each have different watering requirements. Cacti can survive in much drier environments than succulents, while succulents cannot thrive in drought. So, to make sure they both have their needs met, choose a patch of land with direct access to the sun and soil that drains properly.

Make sure to separate the two beds housing the plants. While cacti prefer sandy soil, succulents favor a slightly heavier environment with more oxygenation and a slightly higher demand for irrigation.

As mentioned before, not all cacti are the same, and neither are the succulents. Make sure that the types you're planting together can tolerate the weather and environmental conditions in the area.

When choosing the container, go for a bigger one to make room for both separate beds, allowing room for the growing roots. Make sure your container has holes to drain any excess water and isn't made from material that absorbs it, so go for something like ceramic containers.

Make sure to separate the two beds housing the cacti and the succulents.
https://pixabay.com/photos/cacti-plants-succulents-pots-1845159/

Preparing the Planting Area

When preparing your area for planting, remember that cacti and succulents both do well in mildly acidic soil, with a sandy composition for optimal drainage of excess water.

You can perform a soil test before planting, keeping in mind that the optimal acidic PH balance should range from 5.5 to 5.6.

Depending on the results you get, if they are not within the correct range, you can easily amend the situation by adding sand or humus/girt.

For cacti, having a blend of about 50% sand, 25% humus, and 25% grit would be ideal. Remember, though, that succulents require a heavier growing medium, so maybe increase the percentage of the soil in their section of the bed.

Consider adding organic material to the mix, such as manure or compost.

A viable test for the soil mixture is to wet it and squeeze it tightly with your hands. When you open your hand, the soil should fall apart.

Drainage holes are essential to avoid rotting and withering plants.

If you're planting outside or inside, make sure that the soil is loose and properly aired using a gardening fork. After you've done that, spread a layer of mulch on the surface to reduce weed growth and keep it moist.

It is advised to start preparing the soil 14 days prior to planting. For succulents, try choosing areas with a proper sun-to-shade ratio.

Clean out any weeds, debris, or overlooked pests from previous plantations from your planting area. These unwanted additions to the soil can hinder plant growth or cause irreparable damage.

When placing rocks around your cacti and succulents, you will need to be strategic. Adding a top layer of smaller decorative rocks doesn't just look good but also allows for the soil to retain the heat. This sort of heat retention comes in handy during colder weather to support the sun-loving plant.

Big rocks also act as deterrents to predators, such as medium-sized animals (dogs and deer), from stepping on them and crushing them.

Make sure the ground around your outdoor garden is level to avoid water pooling.

If the area where you are located is known for cold winters with excessive moisture, consider moving your cacti and succulents under an overhead roof or under transparent/translucent coverings to keep them dry.

Planting Techniques

Whether it's growing from seeds, propagation, plant cuttings, or transplanting succulents, there are specific steps you need to follow to be successful.

Transplanting Cacti

- Make sure you have thorn-proof gloves or even kitchen tongs to protect your hands from cacti thorns.

- Another method of keeping safe is wrapping newspaper layers around the prickly bits of the cactus that you plan to move. Five or six layers should keep you safe from any injuries.

- When attempting this, make sure the weather is appropriate. The sunnier, the better, so springtime to early fall is a good time.

- Check and make sure the roots of the plant are completely dry before you move it.

- Dig a hole in the ground around the same depth and width to match the one the potted cactus is in.

- To loosen the soil in the original pot, tap lightly on and around it.

- Carefully and gently remove the cactus from the pot with a shovel with as little disturbance to the roots as possible.

- If the sand mixed in with the soil falls apart in the move, use it to backfill the hole to which you're adding the cactus.

- Use tongs when handling the cacti to avoid injuring yourself, as gloves offer little protection against spines.

- Backfill the hole with the appropriate mix of soil for cacti (mentioned above) until it is right above the roots.

- Add a layer of gravel or lava granules on top of your soil around the cactus.

- Leave the plant for a week before attempting to water it.

Propagation of Indoor Cacti

The use of pups (baby cacti or offshoots of the cacti) not only allows you to increase your succulent population – but also improves the overall health of the parent plant.

Offshoots usually occur at the base of the cacti, and they share nutrients and water with the main plant. Sometimes, they may occur on the body of the cactus, whether that be the stem or the pads.

Here is how propagating works.

- Make sure you have protection gloves, cactus soil mix, alcohol pads or spray, a sharp knife, rooting hormones, and a pot, of course.
- Make sure you clean the knife with the alcohol and then leave it out to dry.
- Put on your protective gloves to avoid injuries.
- Choose the offshoot or pup you wish to propagate, and using the knife, cut at the base where it connects with the parent cactus. Angle the knife at 45 degrees so that the resulting cut firms up quickly before the rot sets in.
- Do not pot the pup right away! Leave it out to dry completely for up to a week, allowing it enough time to callus or dry out.
- Add the cactus potting mix to the pot.
- Insert the cut end of the offshoot into the rooting hormone and then press it gently into the top of the pot.
- Leave it out in the indirect sunlight and add droplets of water to it often.
- Within four to six weeks, your cactus should have grown strong roots.

Growing Cactus from Seeds

Growing from seeds can take a long time and requires a lot of patience. The seeds used to plant cacti come from the flowers that sprout from an adult plant.

Because some cacti never really develop any flowers, opting to buy your seeds from a commercial shop may be the only option.

Cacti seeds may require stratification. This is a process in which a simulation is performed to make it seem as if the seeds have experienced winter before starting the planting process.

Stratification occurs by placing the seeds in a wet brown deposit that doubles as soil called "Peat." Peat is formed from the partial decomposition of vegetable matter in wet, acidic conditions, muddy ground called "bogs," and flooded areas of land called "fens." Peat is often dried out and repurposed for gardening and fuel needs.

After placing your seeds in moist peat, they are placed in your cooler for about four to six weeks until they crack open.

After this process is concluded, make sure you have a cactus soil mix available. Plant the seed in the pot with the mix at an equal depth and width. Cover up the pot with plastic after watering it lightly and place it in a bright location but out of direct harmful sun rays.

Sprouting usually occurs within three weeks, and the covering can be removed during the day after that. After about six months, little seedlings are ready to be repotted.

Planting Cacti Outside

If you're going to choose to have your prickly plants outside, here are the steps to follow:

- Make sure the soil is well prepared with the right cactus mix.
- Make sure the hole you're digging in the ground is as equally deep as it is wide. It should be about one and a half times as wide as the cactus's root ball or stem.
- Set the plant facing north. The north side of the plant usually has an obvious mark on it. If there isn't a mark, make sure you ask about it in the plant store prior to leaving. Why should you do that? Because the plant's south side is most likely placed more in the sun and develops tougher skin than the north side. Incorrect placement may cause the north side to receive more sunlight than it can withstand.
- Backfill the hole with the soil mix and pat it gently afterward.
- Add small amounts of water.
- If you are replanting a cactus bred in a greenhouse, cover it up with a light cloth to shade it from direct exposure to the sun for a couple of weeks.

Planting Cacti and Succulents Together

Before planting, make sure that you've chosen the right combination of cacti and succulents that complement each other visually and can be sustained together in a common environment.

If you're going for a cactus that can thrive in bright sunlight, don't choose a succulent that can easily burn from sun exposure, such as the string of hearts or the snake plants.

Make sure your container is wide enough for both plants to exist comfortably together and has enough room for root growth. Leave about six inches of space between them to allow a healthier co-existence.

And now, on to the repotting process:

- Make sure you've watered your cacti and succulents two days prior to transplanting to the new pot. As the plants are placed in new soil, they need time to adjust to their new environment, so it's best not to water them at all for the first two weeks after repotting. Watering beforehand allows your plants to take their fill of water, and the wet soil makes it easier to remove the roots from the pot.

- Prior to adding the cactus or the succulent, take a closer look at each plant. Make sure that you've checked for any signs of rot, pests, or disease indications. If the plants are left without treatment and joined together in one pot, the infected plant will spread its illness to the rest. Cut off any damaged parts and prune the plants if needed.

- When arranging the plants, pick the design you like. You can go for taller plants at the back and shorter ones at the front, for example.

- You can arrange the planter from the middle. Maybe add your biggest plant and rotate the rest around it.

- A vital thing to remember is that when planting your cacti, leave either one-third or half of the root exposed and unburied and cover it up a bit later on. For succulents, you need to make sure to cover all the roots, as they need more moisture than cacti. When you follow this technique and leave some of the cacti roots above the soil, you avoid overwatering them since they need less water than succulents.

Arranging the Plants for Visual Harmony

There are several ideas to explore when arranging your resilient plants individually or together. Each person has their own taste, and each arrangement can vary dramatically according to the weather and what you're pairing it with.

Here are a few simple ideas for your indoor and outdoor arrangements:

- If you're planting only succulents, try adding different colors and shapes close together to create a tapestry.

- Suppose you're looking for specific themes for your garden. In that case, you can create your botanical masterpiece with the inspiration of life under the sea. Pick out colors that match undersea plants and creatures and start arranging them in the form of coral reefs.

- Try writing words with your plants by planting them in wooden frames of letters.

- You can try adding your plants to baskets instead of pots. For example, forest cacti are famous for their huge flowers, which makes them ideal for individual displays.

- You can add the succulents in two varying sizes and colors in a landscape with a pathway surrounded by white pebbles.

- You can add crevices of rocks to your garden and make it look like the cacti and succulents are sprouting directly from them.

- You can emphasize the look of the garden by raising the soil where your plants are situated to draw the eye toward them.

- Consider filling the nooks in your stone walls with soil and tucking your plants into them. Maybe throw in colorful stones to make the colors more vibrant.

- Try creating a Zen garden. Instead of small rocks and pebbles, add big, flat ones as a base for your cacti pots. Spread smaller rocks between the pots to make it resemble a Japanese garden. Try mixing and matching the color of the plants with the pots and rocks to create the aesthetic you're looking for.

- You can improvise the design of the fence around your home. Instead of wooden planks, you can replace them with cacti. You can plant your succulents along the pathways to create a visual separation between the different areas of your garden. Make sure you add a warning sign next to your plants to avoid unintended injuries.

Chapter 4: Watering Wisely: The CORRECT Way to Water Cacti and Succulents

Cacti and succulents are wonderful plants. Their beauty and numerous benefits make them a pleasing plant choice in the home, but often, there is a preconceived notion about how you should water and maintain these plants. Many think succulents and cacti require little to no water, more water than houseplants, or just as much water as houseplants. Some other common assumptions regarding watering cacti and succulents include using regular potting and well-drained soil and watering during dormant seasons. Some of these assumptions are indeed true. However, it is better to be certain to get the best out of your cactus and succulent plants.

Properly watered plants brighten your home in any season, clean the air around you, strengthen your immune system, and improve your mood. Not getting it right can cause enough damage to undo all of your previous efforts, and once it's done, the difference in your plants is obvious. Therefore, you must know how to water your plants correctly.

This chapter will provide information on how to water your succulents and cacti plants properly to avoid over or under-watering. Additionally, you will learn different techniques and the right tools to use. When you put the information in this chapter into practice, you will become a pro on the *dos and don'ts* of watering your cacti and succulents in no time.

Unique Water Requirements of Cacti and Succulents

Cacti and succulents have distinct water needs, which sets them apart from most common plants. Their watering process has helped them flourish in arid areas, semi-arid regions, and areas with little water availability. Therefore, understanding their distinct and peculiar water requirements when you want to grow them in your home is essential to successfully cultivating and caring for these fascinating and resilient plants. Here are the requirements for watering cacti and succulents.

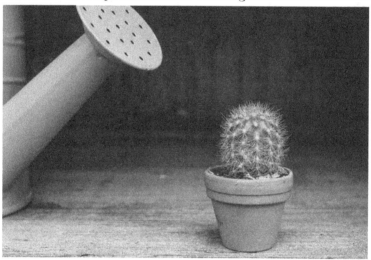

Cacti and succulents have distinct water needs.
https://pixabay.com/photos/cactus-watering-can-houseplant-4161380/

1. Infrequent Watering

Infrequently watering your cacti and succulents is vital to caring for them. Since these plants don't do well in wet conditions, ensure that watering is only done when the soil is completely dry. Avoid initiating a regular watering schedule for your cacti and succulent plants.

Infrequently watering your plants is not the same as neglecting them. When you neglect your plants, they will weaken and whither. Therefore, water your succulents and cacti every fourteen days in summer and every thirty to fifty days during winter.

2. Watering Techniques

Like the watering frequency, the watering technique of succulents and cacti differs from that of other plants. Most plants are watered from top to bottom, but succulents and cacti are watered from the bottom. This makes sure that only the roots get wet and the upper plant stays dry.

3. Drought Tolerance

It's no news that succulents and cacti thrive in areas that some regular plants won't be found in because of their adaptability to arid areas known for their dry and harsh nature. Succulents and cacti possess special tissues for storing water, such as the fleshy stems and leaves, making them tolerant to drought. Thus, you won't be helping them by keeping them wet or damp through a morning and evening watering schedule.

4. Well-Draining Soil

A soil that drains effectively or allows water to flow through freely is another key requirement for watering succulent or cactus plants. A well-draining potting mix should contain materials such as sand, pumice, or perlite, as these elements will prevent water from pooling around the base of your plant. Also, they are a great choice because they help aeration of the soil, which is essential for root health.

5. Rainwater and Water Quality

Rainwater is another requirement for watering succulent or cactus plants. Still, because it isn't always accessible, you can use regular tap water after letting it sit for at least a day. By letting the tap water sit, chlorine and other chemicals evaporate, allowing you to use it to water your plants.

You can also make use of greywater recycling in place of rainwater. Greywater recycling is when household water from the sink, shower, or other parts of the house is reused after appropriate filtration and irrigation.

Furthermore, you can use distilled water. However, distilled water should only be used occasionally because it doesn't contain essential minerals.

6. Seasonal Adjustment

Cacti and succulents are more active during growing seasons like summer and spring. In these seasons, they require extra water. However, more water does not translate to the same amount of water you would use for other plants in your garden. It just means watering should be done more often than normal. Conversely, during seasons like fall or winter, which is their dormant phase, very little water is needed.

7. Observation and Adaptation

There are different species of cacti and succulents, and the distinction in this plant type also means a distinction in their requirements. The specific water requirements of these plants can influence how well they perform. So, after getting them, watch them closely in the first few weeks to work out how much water each plant needs.

8. Plant Environment

The environment where you plant your succulent or cactus also influences how much water they need. For instance, they tend to get dryer when planted in containers rather than directly in the ground. Therefore, if your plant is in a container, it will require more frequent watering than when planted on the ground.

In summary, the special water requirements of cacti and succulents revolve around their ability to store water, their tolerance for dry conditions, and the need for infrequent watering and well-draining soil. Understanding these specific needs and providing appropriate care can help these remarkable plants thrive in your home or garden.

Risks of Overwatering and Underwatering

In the process of watering, many owners of succulents and cacti are unable to get the perfect balance between over and under-watering. This section discusses the risks of under-watering and over-watering these plants.

Risks of Overwatering Succulents and Cacti

Cacti and succulents are built to store water in their tissues, so it's crucial not to overwater them. Overwatering is one of the most common causes of issues with these plants. It's safer to water less frequently when in doubt. Proper watering practices will help your cacti and succulents thrive and prevent potential problems caused by excessive moisture. The following are the dangers of overwatering:

• **Root Rot**

One major effect of overwatering is rotting the roots. Since water is applied to the base of the plant and pools around the base, the roots can be affected by overwatering. When the roots sit in water for too long, they become soft and deteriorate. This rotting process interferes with their natural function, preventing them from absorbing nutrients from the soil properly.

- **Bacteria Problems**

Another problem of overwatering is bacteria multiplication. Microbes multiply in large numbers when plants deteriorate and rot in wet environments.

- **Fungi Problems**

Fungi infestations are a direct problem of overwatering. This problem frequently accompanies root rot, which creates the perfect environment for the emergence of these microorganisms. Fungi infections, such as gray mold and powdery mildew, cause disfiguration and sometimes even death of these plants if the problem is not treated on time.

- **Insect Infestations**

Insect infestation is another key risk brought on by overwatering your cacti or succulents. Certain insects, like thrips or mealybugs, prefer wet areas and love to live on the wet parts of plants. When succulents and cacti are overwatered, bugs or pests infest the cacti or succulents in their weakened state and start reproducing. These insects lay their eggs deep within the plant's tissue, and as they mature, the larvae feed on the delicate interiors of the plant's leaves, flower buds, or stems. After that, infestation takes over, making it nearly impossible to eradicate.

Risks of Underwatering Succulents and Cacti

In the process of watering, many owners of succulents and cacti are unable to get the perfect balance between over and under-watering.

Sreyasvalsan, CC BY-SA 4.0 <https://creativecommons.org/licenses/by-sa/4.0>, via Wikimedia Commons: https://commons.wikimedia.org/wiki/File:Drought_in_a_Lake.jpg

- **Cactus Shriveling**

In the process of preventing over-watering, you could end up under-watering, leaving you with a shriveled cactus plant. Shriveling happens when there is very little water and hydration in your plant's tissues. This dehydration also leads to shrinkage and distorted growth in your plants.

- **The Yellowish Appearance of Cactus**

When cacti are under-watered, they begin to turn yellow. Plants turn yellow when they find it difficult to produce chlorophyll due to damage to the roots of the plants.

- **Cactus Wilting**

One of the many roles of water in cacti is helping maintain the form of the plant. Without enough water within these plants, they start to droop and wilt. However, wilting is more prevalent in cacti or succulents with a more upright and thin posture, which is noticeable when they become soft and unable to hold themselves up.

- **Leaves with Dry Brown Spots**

Dehydration of these plants can lead to brown spots or patches on their leaves. When dehydrated and too close to a heat source or facing direct sunlight, they become susceptible to heat damage and sunburn, which appears as dry brown patches.

- **Brown Patches on the Edges and Tips of Plants**

The tissues of the cactus are meaty, and when the plant is under-watered, brown patches appear around the edges and tips of the plant.

- **Curling of Leaves**

When your cacti or succulents are under-watered, the plant's coping mechanism is to curl up. They do this to save whatever water they have left in them, causing their roots to eventually rot.

- **Weak Spines**

Lack of proper hydration in these plants can result in brittle, weak, and fragile spines. When their spines become weak, they fall off on their own or when touched. As in the case of curled leaves, weak spines can also be a symptom of overwatering.

- **Brittle Roots**

When plant roots are not getting as much water as they should, they become brittle and dry. The lack of nutrients and moisture makes them frail, causing them to break off easily.

How to Determine the Appropriate Watering Frequency

There are several factors to consider when calculating the appropriate watering frequency for your specific succulents and cacti, such as size, plant species, growth stage, soil characteristics, environmental conditions, etc. To determine the appropriate watering frequency, follow the following guidelines:

1. Understand the Species

Succulents and cacti have different sub-species, each with varying water needs. Some are more drought-tolerant, while others require more regular watering. Research the specific water requirements of your cacti and succulent species.

2. Consider Growth Age

The growth age of your plant must be taken into account when watering. If your plant is young, it will require frequent watering, and if it is old, it won't need as much water as the young plant.

3. Evaluate Environmental Conditions

Plants' water requirements and frequency are influenced by their exposure to heat and direct sunlight. Cactus plants require exposure to bright light and warm temperatures, which increases the water evaporation rate. So, ensure your watering schedule is adjusted according to your plant's environment.

4. Check Soil and Potting Mix

Use well-draining soil or a specialized cactus mix to prevent waterlogging and root rot. The soil should allow excess water to drain away quickly.

5. Learn the Signs of Thirst

Pay attention to your cacti and succulents, and watch out for signs of dehydration. Some signs of dehydration include slight wilting, dried spines, root discoloration, or shrinking of the plant. When you notice these signs, water your plants.

6. Perform the Finger Test

The finger test is a cool trick to learn as a seasoned gardener of succulents and cacti. Stick your finger into the soil about an inch (2.5

cm). Pull your finger back up after reaching that depth, and check for signs of moisture. Water only when the soil is completely dry at that depth.

7. Use the Soak and Dry Method

When you water your cacti and succulents, water them thoroughly until the water drains out of the bottom of the pot. Ensure you allow the soil to dry completely before watering again. Avoid frequent light watering, as this can lead to shallow root growth.

8. Water Sparingly in Winter

During the dormant winter months, cacti and succulents require less water. Reduce watering frequency to 30-50 days to prevent overwatering during this period.

9. Avoid Watering the Crown

Water the soil around the base of the plant while avoiding direct contact with the plant's crown (the central part from which the spines emerge). Excessive watering of the crown can lead to the plant rotting.

10. Use a Watering Schedule

Develop a watering schedule based on the specific needs of your cacti and succulents. Keep records to help you keep track and adjust when necessary.

11. Controlled Irrigation

An automated irrigation system provides water at specific intervals, ensuring consistent moisture levels.

How to Choose the Right Watering Tools

When watering cacti and succulents, it's essential to choose the right tools to provide water in a controlled and precise manner. Shown below is a selection of ideal tools for you to choose from.

• Watering Can with Narrow Spout

Choose a watering can that has a long and narrow spout. This type helps you target water directly at the base of the plants. It also helps you avoid getting water on the plant's body or crown, preventing rot or other problems. A watering can with a small capacity is perfect for cacti and succulents, which generally prefer infrequent but thorough watering.

- **Spray Bottle with Fine Mist Setting**

Choose a spray bottle with a fine mist setting that will gently water the small cacti and succulents. It is handy when you're propagating succulents or watering baby plants with delicate foliage. This bottle can also help you avoid overwatering because the mist controls the amount of moisture the plants get.

- **Watering Wand with Adjustable Flow**

Another good piece of equipment to own is the watering wand. This instrument has an adjustable flow for larger cacti, succulents, or multiple plants in the same area. The adjustable flow allows you to control the water pressure, providing a steady stream to reach the entire root zone.

- **Tray and Saucer**

Trays and saucers are necessary for the bottom watering method. This method is a good option for cacti and succulents with sensitive leaves or densely packed spines. It's done by placing the potted plants in a tray or saucer filled with water and letting them absorb water from the bottom up through drainage holes until the topsoil is moist. Empty the tray after some time.

- **Use Well-Draining Soil and Containers**

Use well-draining soil and containers with drainage holes to prevent water from sitting around the roots too long.

How to Assess Soil Moisture Levels Effectively

Knowing a plant's soil moisture is essential for determining when to irrigate. However, it can be challenging to work out when succulents and cacti have accurate soil moisture. You can assess soil moisture properly by using the techniques listed below:

- **Use a Moisture Meter**

Place the moisture meter probe into the soil at different depths to measure moisture levels. This meter will indicate whether the soil is dry, moist, or saturated.

- **Perform the Finger Test**

A finger test is another good way to check for the moisture content of the soil. If the soil feels dry, it needs watering. If it feels slightly moist, it's adequately watered. Saturated soil will feel overly wet.

- **Check the Weight of the Container**

Lift up the container to gauge its weight when watering the plant. Lift it regularly to feel the difference in weight when it becomes noticeably lighter (Wet soil will be heavier than dried soil).

Water Quality and Temperature Considerations

The quality and temperature of the water are both things that need to be checked before you use the nearest water outlet. Not all water is suitable. Here are some factors to monitor.

- **Effects of Chlorine**

Chlorine, a common disinfectant found in tap water, can have detrimental effects on the delicate balance within your cacti and succulents' root systems. It can destroy organisms necessary for plants, thereby damaging plants' roots. Therefore, do not use chlorinated tap water on your succulents and cacti.

- **Effects of Fluorine**

Be on the lookout for fluoride in your water as well. Excessive fluoride levels can be toxic to your plants. Be cautious when you use tap water, not just because of chlorine alone but also for fluoride, as some regions have naturally high fluoride levels. Using filtered water can significantly reduce the risk of fluoride toxicity in your cacti and succulents, promoting their longevity and vibrancy.

- **Excessive Mineral Content**

Water rich in minerals gradually leads to the accumulation of salts in your cacti and succulent soil. This can potentially harm the root systems of your plants. Regular soil flushing is a good way to prevent this build-up. Every few months, water your plants thoroughly, allowing water to flow through the soil and wash away excess salts. This practice will help healthy nutrient absorption and root growth.

Congratulations! With this knowledge, you are well on your way to owning an amazing garden with the best-grown succulents. When next someone talks about a succulent-cacti myth, you'll be able to correct it. Every garden needs succulents and cacti, and not just any kind. Well-grown ones will boost your garden's aesthetics. With your newfound understanding, bring that dream garden to life.

Chapter 5: Cacti and Succulent Health, Care, and Maintenance

Adopting a cactus into your home is usually an effortless process and adds a snap of contrast and color. As they come in almost all shapes, sizes, and colors, blending them in with your decor should not be a massive challenge. Whether you choose to add them to your home, plant them in your garden, or place them on your windowsill, it is crucial to be acquainted with your new house guest's needs. Cacti are known for being tolerant and low-maintenance plants that require almost little to no care. However, a common misconception is that all cacti grow in the desert. That little tidbit is not true. Some cacti actually grow in the forests and are used to living in humid and moist environments. Some cacti can withstand the most arid environments, from the hottest weather to below-freezing cold temperatures.

To be able to properly care for your trouble-free house plant, your best bet is to recreate its natural habitat. Desert cacti can thrive indoors. With the proper care and proactive maintenance, you will be left with a beautiful symphony of colors and unusual formations that please the eye and, in some cases, have healing properties.

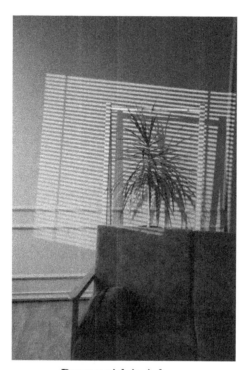

Desert cacti thrive indoors.

https://www.pexels.com/photo/the-sun-shining-through-the-blinds-into-a-room-with-a-sofa-and-a-plant-18246654/

Catching any irregularities in your plant early on prevents complications from becoming a problem. For example, making sure there are no pests or rot in the early stages of growth can prevent problems from spreading to the rest of the plant. In some cases, early diagnosis can protect neighboring plants if it's a tight formation of several cacti or succulents arranged together, whether in a garden or an indoor pot.

As you go through this chapter, you should be able to identify the signs of a healthy cactus versus one that may be struggling to sustain itself. You will find essential information on how to care for and protect your succulent from withering.

Essential Care Practices

There are some basic practices to get you started on the right path to owning healthy and vibrant cacti. Some of these points you may have missed during the initial cactus care. Here are the first things you should check off your list for a hassle-free cacti care routine.

Let There Be Light

After verifying the type of cactus you have and the natural habitat you need to create for it to flourish, consider the amount of light you're exposing it to. Most cacti enjoy bathing in the sun, even indoor plants. Find a south-facing window or corner in your garden to place your cactus. Make sure you don't put it in the direct, hot sun, as that can result in a yellow or brown colored cactus (sun-burned) instead of vibrant green or colorful hues.

If your cactus does turn yellow, try moving it to a place shaded from the light to cool down. Also, don't put it near air conditioning or a strong draft since dry and warm is their love language.

For forest dwelling cacti such as Rhipsalis, you need to provide shade to protect it from direct sunlight, whereas its cousin Echeveria thoroughly enjoys its days in the sun.

In the colder months of the year, around autumn and winter, it's essential to maintain a cool climate of around 46.4°F to 50°F. As the summer and spring roll around, the plants need more air but will be just fine exposed to high temperatures.

Indoor cacti are also known to display quicker growth patterns when placed out during summer nights when the weather is around 122°F.

Make Sure They Are Adequately Hydrated

Cacti are more like camels. They store water for long periods and don't need that much in the first place to survive. There is a fine line between overwatering and underwatering. Each situation has its drawbacks. If you add too much water to your plant, you're delaying and impeding its growth. It can also rot the roots, and your plant could develop scabs that look like oxidized areas on the stem. If you add too little, your cactus will shrivel, wither, and eventually die. Obviously, you don't want that for your greenhouse guest.

A way to check if your cactus is thirsty is by checking the soil. Have a look at the top two to three inches, and if it is completely dry, it's time for a drink of water.

When it comes to watering, if you can, and you have easy access, avoid tap water and use a more natural source, such as rain. That's because tap water contains certain minerals that collect in the soil and are detrimental to your plants. They can also throw the flow of nutrients that the plant relies on into disarray.

Watering during the hot months should be done around once a week. In between watering, you need to make sure that the soil is draining properly and allow it to dry a bit before the next time. If there is excess water that hasn't drained, make sure you empty it.

Watering is a bit more subjective in the colder months, depending on the environment and how fast the soil dries out between watering times. This is a time when the plants enter what is called a resting period. For cacti that flower during the winter, make sure you're providing a warm environment and regular watering. For desert dwellers, you don't need as much water as you think, and they can be left alone for extended periods.

Maintain the Soil

Making sure that the soil drains properly is step one. Making sure your soil is aerated is step two, and maintaining the correct mix of soil, sand, and organic material is the third step towards healthy, happy cacti.

Follow the instructions for your fertilizer to the tee. According to the printed directions, some cacti nutrients need to be diluted before use. As with watering, do not over or under-feed your plant.

Clean Your Plant and Its Surrounding Environment

Every few weeks, take a damp cloth to your cactus and wipe it down to make sure you get rid of any dust or debris stuck to it. Make sure you use protective gear and gloves so you don't come away with a bloody hand.

While most cactus pruning is done to propagate new plants with tiny pups, it is also considered a part of cleaning. Pruning the cactus can be done as a method to control its growth or remove the dead and damaged bits before they spread. This is done using clean and sharp garden shears. As the cactus starts growing, rearrange the rocks you initially added for warmth and protection.

Prevention Strategies for Pests and Diseases

A deterrent to pests and diseases in cacti can come from simply being proactive. Do not wait for your cacti to show signs of ailments that may lead to cutting parts of them off or using harsh chemicals to try to treat them. There are a few techniques that can be followed to prevent pests and diseases.

Inspecting the Roots

Take a close look at the roots of your cacti every two to three months. Some diseases may take months to show physical signs on the plant. You can limit your plant's ordeal by checking its roots, as most problems start from there and work their way up the stem and leaves.

Overwatering

Overwatering your cacti can easily lead to rotting roots. Adding too much water or watering more frequently than needed can be a fertile ground for fungal diseases to grow. So, instead of reaching a point where you need to trim the roots and repot the plant in the hope of saving it, follow the appropriate instructions to water your plant, making sure the soil drains properly.

Maintaining Good Hygiene for Your Plant

Healthy plants are a lot less likely to attract pests and diseases. Ensure you carefully follow the care instructions specific to your cacti species. This includes proper sunlight without overexposure, proper watering techniques, and an adequate soil mix specific to cacti that drains properly. Also, make sure you periodically clean out the pot from fallen leaves and dead flowers.

Quarantine Your New Additions

To avoid the transfer of pests and diseases that may have gone unnoticed before you bought your plants, make sure you separate your new plants from the old ones. Inspect the newcomer's roots and leaves carefully until you're satisfied they are pest and disease-free. If you discover a problem, treat it immediately or dispose of the plant to avoid contaminating the rest.

Make sure you separate your new plants from the old ones.
https://pixabay.com/photos/fat-plants-terracotta-pots-2734948/

Insecticidal Soap

Before you apply this to clean your plant, make sure you read the label very carefully, as some of these are harmful to plants. Check and double-check to make sure that they don't have any negative side effects. Even after you do, only use it on a small part to test it before spreading it over the remaining parts.

Underwatering

Even though you opted for a resilient plant that needs very little water every now and then, it still does need water. Forgetting to hydrate the cacti is a sure way for it to wither and die from the roots up.

Use Organic Fertilizer

Non-organic fertilizers can also be a source of pests and disease. They contain varying amounts of heavy metals like zinc and copper that are harmful to the plants. These fertilizers weaken the plant and leave it vulnerable if it's attacked by pests and diseases. Choose organic fertilizers and foods as much as possible.

Physical Trauma

Treat your cactus gently. When moving it around, potting, and repotting, make sure you don't bump it into any sharp or heavy objects. These physical injuries make it more susceptible to infections.

Be Mindful of the Temperature

Temperature fluctuations can easily affect your cacti, especially if your area doesn't resemble its natural habitat. For example, try moving the cacti inside your home during cold winters to keep it warm and away from the harsh cold. Humidity in the weather can also cause disease, depending on your cacti species. While some thrive in humid weather and grow faster, others may prefer a drier environment to stay clear of fungi and pests.

Soil Mix

As previously mentioned, cacti benefit from a mix of different ratios of soil, sand, and organic material in its soil. However, increase one or the other rather than using a similar mix. For instance, too much sand can easily harm your cactus, making it hard for it to absorb water and nutrients from the soil. Be mindful of the proper mix for your plant prior to planting.

Nutritional Needs and Fertilization

There is more than one option to choose from when it comes to the fertilizer most suitable and safe for the species you're breeding. Whether it is organic or industrial, the first and foremost rule is to follow the instructions. Don't over or under-feed. Don't use fertilizer that could harm the plant. And do not experiment without knowing what you're doing.

The reason you should consider extra nutrients for your cacti is because of the soil composition used for the plant. The mix of sand and easy-draining medium doesn't promote nutrition retention enough, and it's easily washed away before the cactus can benefit from any of it. So, an extra helping hand is needed.

Below, you'll explore the most common and recommended nutritional additives that can benefit your house or garden plants.

Primary and Macronutrients

There are three main macro and primary nutrients that every plant needs to thrive and grow. Nitrogen promotes a healthy stem and foliage, phosphorus for strong blooming and steady, healthy roots, and potassium to assist in absorbing the needed nutrients and to fight off disease.

As you select the fertilizer, you will notice that all of them have the ratio of N-P-K stated on the back of the package. Now, as important as it is to get the right fit and ratio for your plant species, a commonly recommended ratio of the N-P-K is 6-6-6, which usually supports the growth of the cactus.

There are other types where you may find the ratio ranging from 10-10-10 to 20-20-20, which is also not a bad choice, but it may need to be watered down a bit more than the others to avoid over-fertilization and the risk of damaging the roots.

Picking out a fertilizer with added microorganisms improves the conditions in the pot to compensate for the low nutrient levels.

Organic Fertilizer

This is your best choice for fertilizing your cacti. There are quite a few to choose from, depending on your needs.

Compost Manure – If you live near a farm and are growing outdoor cacti, natural animal manure is known for retaining and providing priceless nutrients that benefit your plants.

Whether it's from sheep, cows, or chickens, any of these options should provide you with a green and environment-friendly fertilizer for your plants.

You can use it indoors as well, as long as you keep in mind that the smell may linger a bit longer in a closed space.

Worm Castings - These are basically the manure of worms. This type of fertilizer is rich in humus, improves the ventilation of the cacti soil mix, and balances the pH levels. It is rich in over 60 micronutrients. Along with the N-P-K, they contain amounts of magnesium, carbon, iron, zinc, and many other nutrients. They also assist with absorbing heavy metals from your soil mix, lowering the chance of your plant retaining them in toxic amounts.

Tea Bags - These are little manure tea bags that you soak in water and add to your plants. It comes in the form of biodegradable tea bags. To use these, you need to soak them in about five gallons of water somewhere between 24 and 36 hours until the water turns a golden brown. You then use the water the next time you need to hydrate your plant.

Liquid and Granular Fertilizer

Fertilizers come in many forms: powder, liquid, or granules. Liquid and powder fertilizers are diluted before use on the cacti. The roots easily absorb these nutrients but are unfortunately also washed away easily, so more than one application may be needed for an optimal result.

As for granular fertilizers, they are broken up and spread over the soil mix and then watered in. These types are more concentrated and last for up to nine months. The resulting improvement can be witnessed within two weeks. Make sure that the N-P-K ratio is low to avoid root burn.

Fertilizer Spikes

These, like granules, are considered slow-release fertilizers. They don't make a mess and are hassle-free to use. All you need to do is place the spike in the potting mix at the start of the growth season and water the plant as needed for that species. They also last for nine months and, as they are not visible, they are child and pet-friendly.

Re-Potting and Transplanting

As your plant grows in size or if you wish to relocate a newly bought one, you're probably going to consider re-potting in a new pot. Another reason you may consider this is if the plant was infected with pests or diseases, and you need a clean and fresh reallocation while disinfecting and cleaning its old home. There are a couple of straightforward techniques to take into account to maintain a healthy cactus and to perform the repotting successfully.

A pot with holes in its base to drain the excess water is the best option. Good drainage protects the cactus roots from rotting. However, that doesn't completely rule out the idea of using a regular pot; you just need to take a little bit more care when watering it.

Always make sure that the soil is dry all the way down before watering it, and use ¼ cup or ½ cup of water every week or two. This should allow your cactus to be content.

Now for the actual procedure of a healthy repotting;

- Make sure your plant is watered well before the procedure and properly drained from any excess.
- As you remove the cactus, use protective gloves and folded paper towels to protect your hands.
- Find a way into the old soil using chopsticks to separate it from the roots without damaging it.
- Add the potting mix to the new home and make sure it's slightly wider in diameter, situating your plant on top.
- Add more potting mix and firm down the soil with your hand.
- Keep away from watering for a few days to prevent damaging the roots.

Seasonal Care Adjustments

Caring for your prickly friends differs slightly from one season to another. There are a few differences in watering and placement that should be taken into consideration as colder or warmer weather comes around.

Spring and Summer

As the weather warms up, you should reconsider your watering schedule. If you are in a sunny environment where your plants may be subject to a lot of heat, it is advised to water the cacti once a week. Before watering, make sure the soil is well-drained and dry. Be careful not to burn your cactus by pacing it away from direct sunlight. Place it in a shaded area with enough access to the sun without causing the leaves and stems any discoloring. Also, make sure that the north side of the cactus is facing north, which should be marked beforehand. If you're keeping your cacti indoors, it would be preferable to use a south-facing window. Light is not limited to the sun only, as you can keep it in bright light using indoor lamps.

Autumn and Winter

As the colder months roll around, you may need to cut back on the water a bit. As always, make sure the potting mix has dried out completely between watering. The frequency you choose to water your cactus depends on the weather and environment they are in, along with how different the place they are in is from their natural habitat. Desert cacti and cacti that flower in the winter need different care. While one may thrive on little water and resist the brittle cold, the other may need warmth and extra watering sessions.

Make sure your cacti are well protected from harsh winter drafts, especially if they are indoor cacti or aren't desert dwellers accustomed to colder nights.

Around late February, close to the end of winter, consider sprinkling "Preen," a weed preventer that makes the weeding task much less arduous.

Chapter 6: Pruning and Shaping Stunning Succulents

Succulents require routine upkeep because they grow slowly and eventually outgrow their containers. If you notice that your once neatly cultivated succulents look unkempt, it's time to get out the pruning shears.

Pruning and shaping succulents is not a complex matter. You need to know just a few details to make the process smooth. This chapter will guide you on what this process is, what the benefits are, and the tools and safety precautions needed for the work. Furthermore, you will learn some techniques and how to manage overgrowth and pruning for succulent health and beauty, which, in the long run, will extend the life of your plants.

Pruning and Shaping

Pruning is removing or cutting off a part of the succulent plant, vine, or tree that is not needed for growth or is dangerous to the overall health and development of the plant. Conversely, shaping is a specialized form of trimming focused on designing and maintaining the unique form of the succulent plant. Its application is seen especially in topiary, pollard, etc. In horticulture, pruning, and shaping maintain and boost the plants' growth pattern, size, health, and overall appearance. This is carried out to enhance your plant's growth, and it is an efficient way to maintain developing and established succulent plants. It also occasionally helps protect people, properties, and plants from disease, pests, or damage. This is a long-term maintenance technique.

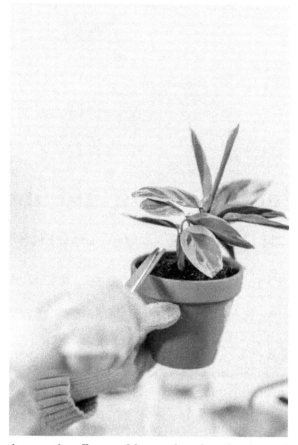

Pruning is removing or cutting off a part of the succulent plant, vine, or tree that is not needed for growth or is dangerous to the overall health and development of the plant.
https://www.pexels.com/photo/a-plant-on-a-clay-pot-9414306/

Benefits of Pruning and Shaping

Promoting Branching: Pruning and shaping to remove or cut off any stagnant branch encourages new growth, leading to a more robust and beautiful succulent plant.

Maintain Plant Health and Aesthetic: When you remove dead, decayed, or diseased parts of succulent plants, it stimulates the aesthetic appeal and the overall health and appearance of the plant. The removal of the dead leaves closes the door to any and every secondary attack of pests.

Controls Growth: Growth control entails pruning the overall size and density of the plant. Shaping, in this case, is used to create a shape for your plant that is pleasing to the eye as well as good for the plant.

Create Distinct Forms: This technique enables you to create unique, specialized designs like topiaries, espaliers, pollards, and hedges.

Encouraging Symmetry: Creating uniformity and enhancing symmetrical appearance through this technique increases the overall visual appeal of the succulent.

Encourage Flower and Fruit Production: Pruning and shaping succulent plants, shrubs, and trees improves the production of fruit and flowers. This is done to stimulate an open canopy to penetrate more light, encouraging the production of a flower bud.

Tools and Safety Precautions

Apart from maintaining the beauty of your landscape, pruning and shaping is vital to promote the health and growth of your succulent plants. The right tools are necessary to get the best results. Below is a list of must-haves, essential tools, and equipment used for this task:

Pruning Shears

Pruning shears are the most frequently used tools for shaping a tree's flowers, shrubs, vines, and minor growths. Pruning shears are designed to be hand-held and can cut up to ¾ in sticks and tree branches. Pruning shears come in three types: ratchet, anvil, and bypass.

Ratchet pruners are like the anvil but were designed to cut in stages. It is a good fit, especially when you don't want to stress your wrist. The anvil pruner has a straight blade that can split dry branches and stems. A bypass pruner is the most well-known among the three and functions like scissors.

Loppers

Loppers are needed to prune and shape vines, nuts, and fruit trees. They can cut branches to the range of 2 1/2 inches thick. Loppers are similar to hand shears, but the blade is thicker, while the handle is very long. Like the pruner, loppers also come in three styles.

Pruning Saw

A pruning saw comes in different sizes and is great for pruning branches ranging from 1 to ¾ in diameter. Folding the pruning saw makes carrying it around your farm or garden easy. The pruning saw is different from the handsaw or hacksaw you see in department stores. It has a curved, narrower, and pointed blade that can easily remove branches when used in a dense environment. The teeth on the pruning saw are well-placed, which causes the saw to cut either way, whether you are pulling or pushing.

Pole Saw and Pole Pruner

You know those small tree branches that are challenging to reach? Well, a pole saw can reach them and cut them. It's safer to prune from the ground instead of using a ladder, and a pole saw gives you that leverage to prune and shape safely from the ground. A pole saw is a saw blade joined to a long pole. A pole pruner, on the other hand, comprises a fixed hook and hung blade controlled by a rope and attached to a long wooden pole. You can cut branches up to 2 inches in diameter using a pole saw and pole pruner.

Thorn-proof Leather Gloves

Some succulents can literally be a thorn in your hand, no matter how pretty or harmless they might seem. Nonetheless, you don't have to dress like you're going to a beehive to get some honey to tend your succulent plants. Scratches and cuts from succulent plants with sharp edges can be prevented by using thorn-proof leather gloves that protect you up to your elbow from being hurt by thorns.

Protective Goggles

These goggles might be big, looking all-nerdy, but on the bright side, they are the very thing that protects your eyes from spider webs, insects, and other foreign bodies. They also protect against poisonous chemicals that get released into the air and nasty allergenic plant pollen. These dangerous substances could lead to problems when they come in contact with your eyes, hence a need for protective goggles.

Step-by-Step Pruning Techniques

Pruning is a vital part of ensuring the health of your plants, and a proper technique is a plus to accomplish this. Here are some step-by-step succulent pruning techniques.

Tip Pruning

Tip pruning, also known as pinch pruning, is the removal of the end of each shoot during the growing season, either with a thumb or a finger on less woody shrubs. At every point where a cut is made, tip pruning nurtures the growth of more shoots at that cut point, leading to a more rounded, succulent plant with more flowering stems. Furthermore, tip pruning gives succulent plants a round, light trim to restore their shape after flowering. To accomplish tip pruning, especially on larger jobs like topiary, use sharp shears or hedge trimmers to give you distinct lines.

Stem Pruning

Stem pruning removes or cuts off distinct branches or stems from the succulent plant. This technique is also used on some herbaceous plants, shrubs, and trees. When and how you use this technique is determined by factors like your desired outcome, the species of plant, and their growth pattern.

Selective Leaf Removal

As the name implies, selective leaf removal is the practice of removing leaves from the stem of succulent plants, especially around areas with clusters of fruit. Selective leaf removal on a succulent encourages air circulation, exposes fruit to more sunlight, enhances insecticide penetration, and reduces herbaceous pH and potassium. Furthermore, it enhances the plant's bud fertility and color. While using the selective leaf removal technique, you must leave some leaves on the stem to encourage the production of more carbohydrates to aid fruit development, growth, and overwintering reserve development. Removing three to four leaves is often enough to achieve this technique.

Shaping Methods

Shaping methods are ways of making definite plant designs. The focus of shaping your succulent plants is to show their beauty and enhance the landscape, allowing farmers or gardeners a little creativity and artistry here and there. Below are some different shaping methods.

Topiary

Topiary is the act of training and pruning your succulent plants, trees, and shrubs into a decorative shape. It is a method where you diligently trim the succulent plant into a pyramid, ship, animal, cone, or any form of imaginative design you choose. Topiary shapes are a good way of adding unique shapes to your garden. It doesn't matter if they are found in a steel container outside your house or among perennials in an enclosed environment. They are the statement plants of your garden.

Topiary is the act of training and pruning your succulent plants, trees, and shrubs into a decorative shape.

Here is how to shape the topiary.

- To shape a ball, get a length of garden wire and construct it into a circular shape that you can hold easily. Then, move it over the succulent plant you want to shape. Make the sphere frame smaller than the foliage's mass if you want a perfect shape.

- To restore a cone shape, stand over the plant and start shaping from the center, working your way outwardly around the plant. As you work, you can rest a cane on each side of the plant to form the shape as a guide for cutting. Fasten the canes at the top to form a wigwam shape, and with a garden wire, bind the sides together. Use your shears to shape the plant within this framework. Using this technique, use a handheld trimmer that looks like sheep shears to get maximum results. It will give your work a clean finish.

Espalier

An espalier method is used to train your succulent plants, especially the ones with fruit, to rest against a support such as a fence or a wall, with various tiers of horizontal branches and a central vertical stem. To create these tiers, you will have to do your first pruning soon after planting and continue to do it annually in summer to keep the plant and its fruit in good shape. The Espalier method is mainly used to train plants to grow against walls or in smaller gardens to maximize space.

An espalier method is used to train your succulent plants, especially the ones with fruit, to rest against a support such as a fence or a wall.

https://pixabay.com/photos/espalier-facade-building-decoration-5032964/

Bonsai

Bonsai shaping is the method of growing and training your succulent plants, shrubs, and trees in a box or container until they become full-sized, mature trees in a mini form. This practice is from China, and its focus is to create a well-balanced, appealing design of trees in a limited area of space. A bonsai must be pruned as often as possible, and it involves two types of pruning: maintenance bonsai pruning and structural pruning. These two processes are vital to bring the bonsai into the desired shape and keep this shape for a long time.

Bonsai shaping is the method of growing and training your succulent plants, shrubs, and trees in a box or container until they become full-sized, mature trees in a mini form.

https://pixabay.com/photos/bonsai-azaleas-rhododendron-3125722/

- **Structural Bonsai Pruning:** Using pruning, you can create a beautifully shaped bonsai succulent. Unlike the maintenance cut of bonsai, structural pruning is more radical and requires you to be well-grounded and prepared. Structural trimming usually occurs at the bonsai's early developmental stage.

- **Maintenance Bonsai Pruning:** This technique aims to maintain the definite style of the plant while promoting its existing shapes in small, easy-to-achieve steps.

Managing Overgrowth and Legginess

Succulent plants need to be pruned every few years. They become overgrown and leggy when not properly tended. So, how do you manage overgrowth and legginess?

Strategies

- **Take Stock of Your Plants:** You will suddenly realize how well some plants are doing compared to others struggling with overgrowth. Take note of your plants and their current state. Move plants around so that each plant has the best growing conditions you can provide.

Causes

- **Normal Growth Pattern:** The plant's growing conditions affect it both positively and negatively. When your plants are supplied with enough nutrients, water, soil, and sunlight, they will grow normally and healthily. On the other hand, when the growing condition becomes 100% perfect, there is bound to be an overproduction of foliage, so much so that the young roots and stems cannot support it. It gives rise to leggy growth and weak plants. This can be frustrating for a gardener who has invested time and effort. No gardener wants to see their cactus plant looking sick.

- **Inadequate Light:** When exposed to low light, plants cannot photosynthesize and make the glucose required for their growth. Hence, the leaves and stems of the plant move upward in search of light. This stretching is what is known as leggy growth.

- **Rapid Growth:** The high nitrogen content in some fertilizers causes vibrant plant growth. Nonetheless, excess nitrogen in the fertilizer can cause rapid, tall, and skinny-looking plants, producing poor flower and fruit yields. Furthermore, rapid growth makes your plant top-heavy, unable to support itself, and more prone to disease.

- **Lack of Pruning:** Plants need pruning at one point or another to remove too many dead leaves and leggy growth. If you want to foster thicker, sturdier branches and stems, it is best to prune your plants early during spring. Your plant's health will diminish if leggy stems are neglected.

- **Nutrient Imbalance:** A nutrient deficiency in your plants leads to poor flower and fruit production and leggy growth. This is why regular fertilizing is a must. Nonetheless, when you fertilize plants too much, it causes leggy growth. The way out is to use a diluted water-soluble fertilizer. Furthermore, stop fertilizing regularly if you are still seeing leggy growth. Let the plant recover by itself.

Corrective Measure

- Put the plant in a deeper container to allow the stem to be completely immersed in the soil. Plants that have hairs on their stem can grow into roots.

- When planting in your garden, ensure the stem is buried completely in the soil. The soil serves as a source of support and provides extra nutrients for the stem.

- Expose your plants to direct sunlight or ensure you have a grow light to enable your plants to photosynthesize easily and make enough food needed for healthy growth.

- Use a good watering system and ensure the soil is drained properly.

- Do not over-fertilize. This is usually the cause of legginess.

- Prune regularly to remove leggy foliage and dead leaves. This will stimulate airflow to lower leaves and prevent plants from giving nutrients to unhealthy foliage.

Pruning for Succulent Health and Beauty

Techniques for Improved Air Circulation

Allowing air to circulate is vital for the overall health and appearance of your succulent plants, and here is how to achieve this.

- **Removal of Dead Leaves**: Remove dead or decaying leaves as you prune. Don't leave them around your plants where they could become home to pests and too much water.

- **Prune Overgrowth and Legginess:** Thin out areas in your garden that are overgrown by removing some leaves, stems, etc.

- **Lift the Pot or Container off the Ground:** This technique allows air to circulate around the pot as you lift it from the ground.

- **Place Your Pots in an Airy Location:** Look for areas with enough air and place your succulent pot there. This will help minimize the risk of damp soil that gives rise to diseases.

- **Avoid Overwatering and Over-Fertilizing:** Over-fertilizing and watering results in leggy growth. Water your plant only when you notice that the soil is dry.

Identifying Signs of Unhealthy Growth or Damage

- **Leaning Towards the Light:** When your succulent plants begin to bend towards the light or lean toward the direction of your window, it means that your plant is in serious need of sunlight.

Move your plant toward a source of light to correct this.

- **Shriveled Leaves:** Dying leaves are normal in the succulent plant world. You may even start pruning your succulent plants by taking out some leaves when they look unkempt. However, when all the leaves begin shrinking, your plant needs water. Firstly, see if the soil is dry. If yes, water your plant, ensuring the soil is well-drenched. Furthermore, keep a schedule for watering your succulent plants.

- **Rotting:** You will know you are experiencing rot when the base of your plant and its leaves get mushy. This is due to too much watering, with the soil becoming waterlogged. Wait for the soil to dry out if you sense that the rot is caused by over-watering. If the rot persists, then you need to consider trimming your succulent.

- **Yellow Leaves**: Yellow leaves are caused by over-watering. Refrain from watering until the soil becomes dry and the leaves start regaining their color.

- **Black or Brown Spots**: If your plant turns black or brown along the trunk or at a certain spot, your watering is slightly over the top. Refrain from watering and observe the trunk, as chances are that the spot will disappear. However, restoring such plants will be difficult if the trunk has turned completely black.

- **Dull Color**: This is caused by too much exposure to sunlight, which results in bleaching. You can see a purple or yellow plant turn lighter green or a green succulent turn white or pale green. Moving your plant away from sunlight to a less-bright corner can help in this situation.

Pruning and shaping is one of the most daunting and misconstrued landscape maintenance strategies for homeowners, farmers, and gardeners, and most individuals don't know what to do or how to do it. Understanding what this technique entails and which tools to use should clear up some confusion and fears you may have had on how to manage the overgrowth of your succulents. Take your time to observe your plant and act accordingly.

Chapter 7: Propagation Techniques and Maximizing Yield

Grown, nurtured, and pruned your very first succulent species to your heart's desire? Great work! Do you wish you could collect more of the same plant, down to its genetic makeup? Your wish will be granted in this section. Welcome to the fabulous and intriguing world of propagating cacti and succulents, where the science of gardening meets the magic of creation.

Propagation is the reproduction of plants. As a gardener, aspiring or experienced, you may already know that plants generally reproduce through pollination. It is the process of merging two parts of different flowers - pollen grains of the male with the stigma (central part) of the female - to produce the offspring (seeds).

Propagation is the reproduction of plants.
Propagation at Peckover by Barbara Carr, CC BY-SA 2.0
<https://creativecommons.org/licenses/by-sa/2.0>, via Wikimedia Commons:
https://commons.wikimedia.org/wiki/File:Propagation_at_Peckover_-_geograph.org.uk_-
3610104.jpg

It's like a platonic variant of human reproduction in the sense that the two flowers don't mate together. Pollination occurs when an external agent (insects, wind, water, etc.) collects the grains from one flower and drops them in the stigma of the other.

If you have put your thinking cap on, you may have already started imagining how you could enact the role of an external agent to breed your very own batch of succulents. Hold your horses, though, and think some more. Pollination will give you a hybrid, not the same plant with identical DNA.

To duplicate your favorite cactus's genetic makeup, you will need to learn the technique of cloning (yes, it is real, not sci-fi!). To understand that technique better, you will need to ascertain why you should propagate your plants in the first place.

Benefits of Propagation

The propagation of cacti and succulents has a number of personal benefits as well as various ecological advantages. It has a positive impact not only on humans as a species but also on the environment as a whole.

- ## Expanding Your Collection

How many times have you succeeded in growing succulents from seeds? And how many times have you ended up buying a brand new, full-grown plant instead? The next time you wish to expand your succulent collection, you don't need to spend any more money on buying seeds or plants. With propagation, you can fill your backyard with as many cacti and succulents as you want.

- ## Choose What You Grow

Do you want a particular species of cactus or a specific type of hybrid? Plant shops and nurseries usually don't stock every species, and even if they do, they won't have more than one or two on sale. Once you know the art of propagation, you won't ever have to search for your favorite hybrid. Simply grow one from your existing plants, multiply your collection of a particular species, or experiment to develop a new one! Choose exactly the kind of cacti and succulents you want.

- ## Share with Others

Say that you and your neighbor have been growing cacti and succulents for so long that you each have your own comprehensive collection. But you don't both have the same varieties. What if you work together and share your collections with each other? Propagation allows you to do just that. While sharing, you don't incur any losses. You just need to hand over some small part of your plant to them, which eventually grows back.

- ## Save Money

Many kinds of cacti and succulents are priced in the lower bracket. But while expanding your collection, those costs will add up. Propagation is much cheaper and, in certain instances, free. You can save a ton of money in the long run after learning the art.

- ## Prevent Extinction

Quite a few species of succulents are rare, and a few others are hard to grow. Some of them even require very specific conditions to thrive that aren't easily found. All these factors combined may result in the extinction of species like the astrophytum asterias or star cactus. Propagation can prevent their extinction by multiplying them, which is slightly easier than growing them from scratch.

Mastering Propagation Techniques

The benefits of propagation are appealing and may have prompted you to try out this art for yourself, especially if you have grown up watching sci-fi movies like the Star Wars franchise. But before you learn how to clone your cacti and succulents, it's important to understand and master the process of seed propagation.

Seed Propagation

A Fair Warning: It is much easier and faster to buy new seeds than to pollinate them from existing cacti. But suppose you want to create a special hybrid, grow succulents without spending any money, or simply experience the joy of creation. In that case, seed *propagation is the way to go*.

1. Wait for your succulents to mature. It may take anywhere from a year to over 50 years. Once they start blooming, you can begin the process of propagation.

2. It is better to keep the two plants that you're about to pollinate beside each other. For instance, the best way to pollinate a bunny ears flower is to shake the male flower directly over the female stigma of the other plant.

3. Alternatively, you can catch the pollen of the male with a paintbrush. Dip the brush in rubbing alcohol to clean it thoroughly. Rub it over the male flower's center, where you will notice white dust-like dots. That's pollen. Let it get smeared around the entire brush.

4. Bring the brush to the female flower's center, where the stigma is located. Ideally, you will just need to push the brush in lightly to stick the pollen to the stigma. But if it doesn't stick, then it could be that the stigma isn't open yet. Wait for a few days until it opens and the particles stick.

Once the pollen has mated with the stigma, all you need to do is wait. The process may produce seeds within a month, or it may take an entire year. Then, simply collect the seeds and plant them in a different pot in the same way as described in Chapter 3. You will be able to grow the offspring of the two plants, which may be the same kind of plant or an entirely different hybrid, depending on which seeds you have managed to propagate.

As you may have noticed, seed propagation may take around a year or more to begin developing a new succulent. The cloning process, on the other hand, is much faster and easier.

Stem Cuttings

As the name suggests, cut stems of your cacti and succulents are used to grow new plants. This method has a two-way benefit. You can prune the old plant while growing a new one. Succulent stems grow larger and longer than their leaves to absorb more sunlight. When they reach the point where your ornamental plant starts looking weird and out of place, you can cut the stems and wait for a new one to grow.

But don't throw the old stem cuttings away. You can use them to propagate more of the same kind of cactus or succulent if you want. Here's how you can go about it.

Cut stems of your cacti and succulents are used to grow new plants.
https://www.pexels.com/photo/person-cutting-a-stem-6764325/

1. Ensure that the cut stem is healthy with fresh-looking leaves.

2. Keep the stem as is in your room with enough indirect sunlight for a couple of days or more. That way, it will callus, and the part where it was cut will become dry, keeping rot at bay.

3. Pour damp cactus or succulent soil into a fresh pot. Just to refresh your memory, cactus soil has more inorganic sediments, whereas succulent soil has more organic ones.

4. Insert the cut stem into the soil with the callused part in the soil. If there are leaves on the sides, it may not go in. Pluck them off, but only those near the base.

5. Place the pot in indirect sunlight, say on a porch with a roof.

6. Water the soil and wait for a couple of weeks. From here on, you only need to mist the soil if it dries up, which may happen after a week or so.

7. Continue misting until you can see roots forming in the callused stem. It may take a month or even a whole year.

8. Once roots have begun to form, you can water and care for your newly grown cacti and succulents, as shown in Chapters 4 and 5.

You can try changing the rooting medium from soil to water, but there is a much higher chance that the stem may rot while submerged in water. For a better success rate, stick with cactus and succulent soil.

Despite healthy soil containing the required nutrients and enough water, is your stem still showing no roots after several months? You can try to kickstart the process by using rooting hormones. They are available in powdered or liquid form, consisting of natural auxins that prompt your stem to initiate root growth.

Stem cuttings produce genetic clones of your cacti and succulents, but that's not the only way that you can propagate or clone your plants. Leaves can also be used for the same purpose.

Leaf Cuttings

Similar to stem cuttings, the cut leaves of your succulents are used to grow new plants. This type of propagation isn't applicable to cacti since they don't contain any leaves. Cloning through leaf cuttings is one of the fastest types of propagation since you can expect new roots in around two months. The process is just like that of stem cuttings, with barely any deviations.

1. Choose the succulent that you want to duplicate. It must contain enough moisture in the sense that its leaves don't feel dry and shriveled.

2. Pluck a fresh leaf from the bunch, one that feels healthy and fleshy. A simple pull won't do the trick. You will need to twist the base of the leaf slightly before pulling it out.

3. You may notice some wetness on the plucked part, which is good since it implies that it has enough stored water to be fresh and healthy. Before you can push it into the soil, you will need to dry it. Let it lie on a dry surface for about two days, at least until you can notice calluses at the base. It may even take up to five days.

4. Pour the succulent soil into a pot and keep it damp before inserting the leaf, callus down, into it.

5. Place the pot in indirect sunlight and wait for a couple of weeks.

6. Take the leaf out and check the base. Can you see small threadlike roots down there? If not, you may need to wait another week.

7. After another few weeks, you will notice small versions of your succulent plant growing from those roots.

8. There will come a time when the original cut leaf falls off. That is when you have to unearth those baby succulents and plant them in a fresh drainage pot with a hole in the bottom.

If roots or baby succulents aren't developing, you may try dipping the callused part of the leaf in rooting hormones. Water rooting medium isn't recommended for leaf cuttings since they may quickly rot.

Division Propagation

Remember those sci-fi films of yore where a human is symmetrically cut into two parts, after which the symmetrical parts are regenerated to form two of the same human being? That is somewhat how division propagation works in cacti and succulents. You simply need to divide a single plant into multiple segments. Each segment contains all the necessary parts of the plant, right from its leaves down to its roots. Here are the basic steps of division propagation for your cacti and succulents.

1. Take a cactus or succulent and separate it from the soil. In many plants, you can easily pick out individual, divided segments with seemingly isolated parts. In those where the segments aren't readily apparent, you will need to tear the plant into small clumps.

2. Pour cactus or succulent soil into a drainage pot and dampen it a bit. Dig a long hole in the middle.

3. Insert the plant segment/clump into the hole and cover it with soil in such a way that the roots lie beneath the surface.

Eventually, a new cactus or succulent with the same genetic makeup will start growing in the pot.

A Point to Note: It is not possible to divide all species of cacti and succulents. Your plant needs to have one of three things to qualify for division propagation.

- It should have multiple tiny stems instead of a single stump. It is easier to separate the roots in that way.

- Has your succulent given rise to smaller (baby) succulents on the side? They are called offsets, and they are perfect for division propagation.

- Have you planted two or more cacti in the same pot? Once fully grown, it is a great time to separate them into different pots through division propagation.

Handle the separate clumps with care, and make sure that none of their parts fall off during the transfer.

Now that you know the steps of every propagation technique and have mastered cloning cacti and succulents like an expert gardener, it's time to learn how to maximize your yield.

Maximizing Yield with Propagation

Do you want a good number of seeds or baby succulents from a single round of propagation? Do you want your yield to be lush and healthy, as if your cactus has been picked afresh straight from the desert? Follow these tips to maximize your yield during and after propagation.

- **Ensure Proper Nutrition**

Cacti and succulents get most of their nutrition from the soil itself, and since they thrive in a harsh, dry environment, you don't need to fertilize them as often as other plants. Fertilization only ensures that the plant can adapt to your home environment more easily, along with increasing the possibility of growing offsets if they are able to. Giving them the required nutrients once a year is enough.

For potted succulents, you may feed fish emulsion or manure tea. Ideally, any 5-10-5 fertilizer will work (for both cacti and succulents), where five is the amount of nitrogen, 10 is phosphorus, and the last five is the level of potassium. Of these, nitrogen ensures the healthy development of stems and leaves, whereas phosphorus focuses on the growth of flowers and roots. Make sure you dilute the fertilizer in some water because a concentrated dose may cause rot.

- **Provide Sufficient Exposure to Light**

Cacti and succulents can live for long periods without water and nutrition, but they need light to survive for even a short while. It's a no-brainer because these plants have adapted to drought areas with scorching heat and light. It is recommended that you keep your pot exposed to direct sunlight for at least six to seven hours each day. For outdoor planting, pick a spot where sunlight falls most of the day.

If you are planning to plant indoors in some dark corner of the room, then pot a plant that can survive without much light exposure. For example, the snake plant can flourish without direct sunlight in a semi-dark room for a long time. Its delightful appearance also improves your interior decor, and it purifies the air.

However, suppose you are bent on planting a light-requiring cactus or succulent indoors where there isn't sufficient sunlight. In that case, you may use artificial light for the purpose. You will need a mixture of fluorescent light and incandescent light in the ratio of 10:1. It means if you have a 10-watt fluorescent lamp, you will also need a 1-watt incandescent bulb. Keep these light sources on for 16 hours each day.

• Keep the Temperature in Check

You may think that cacti and succulents only survive in high-temperature environments. That is not true. Did you know they can do well in temperatures as low as 40°F? That is because the nights in the arid lands are often cold, so they have adapted to survive in varied temperature conditions. Problems may arise if the temperature falls below 30°F.

Do you have prolonged winters with lots of snow in your area? Don't be disheartened, as you can still grow and care for your plants in extreme cold. Place a burlap film covering the plant, ensuring it covers it completely. That will protect it from the direct chill while letting in enough direct sunlight through the pores.

Additionally, avoid watering your cacti and succulents in the winter because they exhaust their supply slower than usual. Pour water only if the soil has dried out or the plant has hardened due to lack of water.

• Maintain the Required Humidity

Cacti and succulents, like other plants, require humidity to survive, but they need it in smaller amounts. Most other plants have a survival range of 60% to 90% humidity, whereas succulents can thrive in even 10% humidity. Nevertheless, the recommended range for most cacti and succulents is around 40% to 60% humidity.

The amount really depends on one important factor - the thickness of the leaves. The thicker the leaves, the less humidity is needed. But how do the cacti with less thick leaves get humid in a desert, you may ask. They collect it from the fog. If your neighborhood doesn't see much fog during the year, you can give your plant what it needs through the misting process. Simply mist the leaves with filtered water.

- **Ensure Proper Spacing**

If you are a seasoned horticulturist, you may know how critical spacing is for efficient succulent growth. Are your garden cacti planted too close to each other? They will use up more water and nutrients than usual and may need more than six hours of sunlight.

The thing is, when plants are clumped too close together, they tend to compete for the basic requirements. And where there is competition, there's a winner and a loser - fundamentals of Charles Darwin's survival of the fittest. Thus, some of your plants in a crowd may thrive while others may wither away.

It is recommended that you space your cacti and succulents at least two feet apart. Large plants, like saguaro, which can grow quite wide and tall, will need more space of around four to five feet between them.

In short, to maximize the yield of cactus and succulent propagation, you must expose them to six hours of direct sunlight, keep the temperature above 40°F, and ensure two to three feet of spacing between two plants. Nutrition and humidity can be naturally acquired, but you may provide your plants with them to boost healthy growth.

Chapter 8: Pest Control, Disease Management, and Other Challenges

Just like humans need adequate care and disease management to stay healthy, succulents and cacti require pest control and proper disease management to remain healthy and thriving. Although cacti thrive well while there is limited water availability, they still need protection against pests and several diseases. These pests and diseases can affect their distinct appearance and compromise their growth.

Mealybugs, scale insects, whiteflies, spider mites, vine weevils, and caterpillars are commonly found pests that affect succulents and cacti. These pests primarily feed on plant tissue, disrupting the nutrient distribution within the plant and even transmitting harmful microorganisms that develop into diseases. Identifying and getting rid of pests early on is vital for your plants to survive.

Several fungi, viruses, and bacteria also affect cacti and succulents. These microorganisms cause diseases including leaf spot, stem rot, root rot, and other fungal infections. Most of the time, cacti's main culprits are poor conditions such as high humidity, poor air circulation, excessive fertilizer use, and overwatering.

Avid gardeners recommend using a holistic approach where prevention is the first line of defense. Providing the proper humidity, water, and sunlight and keeping the soil well-drained will ensure your cacti flourish and stay protected from diseases. Besides giving your plants a suitable growing environment, inspecting them regularly for any signs of disease or pest infestation is necessary.

A reasonably novel approach called Integrated Pest Management (IPM) is used chiefly to address pest infestations and diseases. This management method combines cultural, mechanical, biological, and chemical controls. Natural methods include pruning and handpicking pests. Chemical control involves using insecticides and fungicides, and mechanical methods involve using specific equipment to avoid harmful effects.

Common Pests That Affect Succulents

There are several pest species capable of disrupting the growth of cacti.
https://pixabay.com/photos/leafhopper-insect-macro-nature-562118/

There are several pest species capable of disrupting the growth of cacti. The detrimental effects a pest infestation might have on the plant depends on the type of pest and the severity of the infestation. Here are some common problems, how to identify them, and ways you can prevent this infestation.

Mealybugs

These small, soft-bodied insects are covered in a white, waxy, cotton-like substance that provides protection. They cluster on the plant's stems, base, and leaves. These bugs are oval and can range from a millimeter to four millimeters. With multiple legs, mealybugs have a white-colored waxy outer coating. This coating gives mealybugs their distinct cotton-like appearance. You'll see clusters of cotton-like substances on the leaves, stems, and base, where the plant sap is easily accessible.

Scale Insects

These tiny, oval-shaped insects can attach themselves to leaves and stems, sucking the plant sap and thriving unnoticed. They come in various colors, depending on the scale of insect species, but all have an outer soft body. Scale insect infestation in your cacti garden can turn them yellow or brown. These insects also feed on the plant's sap, sucking their life force (sap) and making your precious plants prone to other diseases. The cacti leaf can also appear as having a sticky appearance.

Aphids

These are small, soft-bodied insects resembling a pear in appearance. Aphids have long antennae and wings and come in different colors, including yellow, green, pink, and brown. These insects infest areas of new growth or the underside of leaves, making them difficult to identify. They also feed on the plant's sap, sucking the life force out of your prickly cacti. Like scale insects, aphids produce honeydew that attracts ants and other insects, increasing the chances of developing fungal infections.

Spider Mites

While spider mites seem like any other insect, they are arachnids, a subcategory of invertebrate animals. Spider mites are primarily brown, red, or yellow and are nearly impossible to identify without magnification tools. Like spiders, they have eight legs and feed directly on plant leaves. The damage spider mites cause results in yellowing of the area. Over time, the plant stops growing and declines even further.

Thrips

These tiny, slender insects have fringed wings that measure less than one millimeter. Thrips are yellow, black, or brown, have elongated bodies, and appear all over the plant. While feeding on the plant's tissue, thrips leave a silvery streak on the leaves. Slowly, your cacti will show distorted or discolored growth. Thrips can carry viral infections and spread disease to other plants.

Whiteflies

These tiny flying insects have white-colored wings containing a powder-like substance released during flight. Their body resembles a moth and has four wings. They reproduce under the leaves, hidden from plain sight. Similar to other insects, whiteflies feed on plant sap and cause wilting. They can also trigger sooty mold growth in the plant.

Fungus Gnats

Gnats are dark-colored flies that look similar to fruit flies. They are more active around the soil surface of potted plants. Their long, slender bodies make them agile flyers. Adult fungus gnats do not cause significant damage to the plants. However, their larvae feed on organic matter in the soil, including plant roots and tender root hairs, which can affect the plant's overall health and growth.

Root Mealybugs

Although root mealybugs look similar to regular mealybugs, this type thrives underground and feeds on the plant's roots. It's nearly impossible to detect their presence until their population becomes massive. Infected cacti show wilting and stunted growth.

Leaf Miners

Leaf miners are mostly larvae of insects like moths, flies, and beetles that feed on the plant's tissue, leaving holes in the leaves. They are worm-like creatures and create tunnels or trails on the leaf surface. These miners also vary in color, ranging from brown to white.

Vine Weevils

These beetles have a distinctive snout and don't fly like regular beetles. Weevils go unnoticed during the day as they are nocturnal.

Identification: Vine weevils are small, flightless beetles with a distinctive "snout." They are nocturnal and often go unnoticed during the day. Vine weevils prefer nutrition from the roots but can also feed on leaves, leaving semicircular notches.

Leafhoppers

Leafhoppers are insects with intricate patterns on their bodies and long hind legs that allow them to jump. They can also cause wilting, stippling, or yellowing leaves. Severe infestations can even inhibit new growth.

Regular inspection, maintaining hygiene, providing the best growth conditions, and controlling pests are the main elements that need to be taken care of. Knowing about diseases and pests is crucial to prevent them from happening. Lastly, start with the least harmful method to protect the cacti and succulents when identifying the pest. For example, if there are a few visible pests, use natural predators like beetles and harvestmen to keep the pest population at bay without affecting the plant. Lastly, when using insecticides, always use controlled amounts and follow instructions carefully for maximum results.

Integrated Pest Management Techniques

This comprehensive pest management technique is one of the most sustainable approaches toward pest control in cacti and succulents. The method aims to reduce insecticide use and incorporate several pest control approaches for an impactful output. Here are the strategies used collectively in integrated pest management.

This comprehensive pest management technique is one of the most sustainable approaches toward pest control in cacti and succulents.
https://pixabay.com/photos/slug-policeman-lego-garden-pest-1535140/

Cultural Control

This practice is a foundational pillar of pest management, focusing on fostering an environment where plants can thrive and build resistance against pests and diseases.

When purchasing the cacti and succulents, inspect them thoroughly for any signs of disease or pests to avoid bringing home infested plants.

Water the plants adequately and avoid overwatering to prevent the development of root-related diseases.

Before planting, ensure the soil is well-draining and the soil mix has adequate fertilizers to keep the cacti nourished. You can let the soil dry out between watering to discourage pest infestations.

Keep your beautiful cacti in places with ample sunlight and ventilation. They won't require direct sunlight, so one of the best places is near windows. Ventilation is crucial to prevent humidity build-up. Humid environments promote the development of fungal infections in plants and provide a feasible environment for pest infestation.

When adding new cacti to your collection, keep the newly bought plant isolated for a few weeks, ensuring no pest or disease infestation could affect other plants.

Mechanical Control

It involves the physical removal of pests from plants. The following mechanical control methods are used to get rid of unwanted pests.

Handpick pests on your cacti and succulents, especially on the undersides of leaves and along the stems, if any. In cases of pest infestation, use a soft brush or a cotton swab dipped in rubbing alcohol to wipe off pests like mealybugs and aphids.

Most pests infest specific areas, like the undersides of the leaves, and should be permanently removed by pruning. Use sharp and sterilized pruning shears to prevent further spread.

Biological Control

The biological method in integrated pest management promotes the use of natural techniques to keep the pest population at bay. Ladybugs and certain beetles can be used to prevent the infestation of mites and several other pests. Similarly, adding nematodes to the soil can control pests like mealybugs and fungus gnats.

Chemical Control

Although chemical control methods are included in IPM, using this as a last resort is strongly advised after you've tried other pest control methods.

Start with the least toxic pesticide and avoid broad-spectrum insecticides that can harm insects living in symbiosis with the cacti. Pay attention to the safety precautions, timing, and application rates, and always use protective gear before application. Instead of spraying pesticides all over the plant, keep them confined to specific areas of infestation, reducing their adverse effects on the cacti.

Adopting the controls mentioned above will keep plants healthy and make pest management effective. Besides using these techniques, make it a habit to inspect your plants regularly so you can act early and stop pest infestations in your cacti collection.

Understanding Succulent Diseases

Although cacti are resilient plants and can thrive in harsh environments, they are still prone to various diseases. Common cacti diseases can result from fungal, bacterial, and viral infections. Knowing the disease's signs and symptoms is necessary for early intervention and effective management.

Fungal Infections

Fungal infections occur in humid environments or when the plant has been overwatered. Some commonly occurring diseases in cacti include the following.

Root Rot

This fungal infection causes wilting, changing the leaf color to brown or yellow. Slowly, the plant loses its ability to grow, and the root system starts turning brown. The root system also becomes rotten and produces a distinct and musty smell. The first sign is the change in the root color, which turns from white to dark.

Stem Rot

The stems affected by stem rot turn black or brown, become sunken, and can even ooze sap. The area gets mushy, which, on closer examination, can reveal discolored tissues. Fungal spores are also visible on the stems when the disease is fully developed.

Leaf Spot

The leaves in this fungal infection become irregularly shaped and develop distinct margins. Concentric leaf patterns can be seen on the leaves, and they turn brown or gray. Fungal spores can also be identified on the leaves when the fungal infection has fully developed.

Bacterial Diseases

Bacterial Soft Rot

Soft lesions start developing on the stems, which can quickly become slimy and mushy. Bacterial soft rot, when developed, has a foul odor that becomes intense as the infection turns severe. Dissecting the affected area can reveal disintegrated tissue that has already lost its functionality.

Bacterial Crown Rot

Bacterial infection limited to the area where the stem meets the roots is known as bacterial crown rot and can damage the plant's integrity. The stem becomes weak, and eventually, the plant collapses. Yellowing or wilting becomes evident as the stem is unable to transport nutrients from the stem throughout the plant.

Viral Infections

Like any other viral infection, they don't have a specific cure. Once a plant is infected, the virus remains in it for its lifetime. Common viral infections include the following:

Cactus Virus X

Mosaic patterns or dark green rings can be seen in cacti affected by cactus virus x. The plant will show stunted growth when infected, and the flowers will fail to open or become deformed.

Acting promptly is crucial during the diagnosis and treatment of a disease. Isolating the infested plants, preventing further spread, providing the right growing environment, and avoiding overwatering are some practical techniques that are beneficial in controlling the disease symptoms.

For most fungal and bacterial infections, isolating and treating the plant with a feasible medication can prevent further spread to nearby plants. However, destroying the infected plant might be necessary for viral infections if the viral infection is severe.

Management of Succulent Infections

Fungal Infections

Improve Drainage: Plant cacti and succulents in well-drained soil. Stagnant water within the soil can create good conditions for fungal growth.

Ensure your cacti and succulents are planted in well-draining soil. Avoid soggy conditions that promote fungal growth and root rot. Use a potting mix specifically designed for cacti and succulents.

Reduce Humidity: Maintain good air circulation around your plants and avoid high humidity. Fungal pathogens thrive in humid environments, so ensure proper ventilation in indoor spaces and avoid overcrowding plants.

Remove Infected Plant Parts: As soon as you identify the first sign of a fungal infection, immediately prune the affected area, limiting the spread of the disease to unaffected parts. When removing the diseased area, use clean pruning shears and disinfect between cuts.

Apply Copper-Based Fungicide: Severe fungal infections require the application of a copper-based fungicide. This fungus-killing substance is effective against a variety of fungal pathogens. Always apply the fungicide on a small area to check for adverse effects, and then use the fungicide on the main affected area according to the instructions.

Bacterial Infections

Practice Sanitation: Keep your growing area clean by removing fallen leaves and debris, as they can harbor bacterial pathogens. Regularly clean your gardening tools with rubbing alcohol or a bleach solution to prevent the transmission of bacteria between plants.

Isolate Infected Plants: Immediately isolate plants that show signs of bacterial infection to prevent the spread to healthy ones. Monitor the isolated plant/s closely and avoid handling other plants before washing your hands and disinfecting tools.

Improve Air Circulation: Maintain adequate spacing between plants to enhance air circulation. Air circulation reduces humidity and decreases the chances of developing bacterial infections.

Remove Infected Plant Parts: At the first sign of bacterial infection, remove and destroy the affected parts, including leaves, stems, or the entire plant if necessary — disinfect pruning tools between cuts.

Viral Infections

Prevention Is Key: Virtually every viral infection affecting plants has no definitive cure. There is no cure for viral infections in plants. The best approach is prevention. Purchase plants from reputable sources and inspect them thoroughly for any signs of viral diseases before adding them to your collection.

Quarantine New Additions: Isolate new plants for a few weeks to observe any symptoms of viral infections before integrating them with your existing collection.

Sanitize Tools and Hands: Disinfect gardening tools by handling different plants to prevent the transmission of viruses. Wash your hands thoroughly before and after handling plants, especially if you suspect an infection.

Remove and Destroy Infected Plants: If a plant shows clear signs of viral infection, such as mosaic patterns or rings on the leaves, remove and destroy the infected plant to prevent the spread to other healthy plants.

In all cases, acting fast when you notice any signs of disease is crucial. Early detection and quick action can significantly improve the chances of successful disease management. For severe or persistent infections, consider seeking advice from a plant expert or horticulturist who may provide additional guidance for your situation.

Remember that maintaining a healthy and disease-free environment for your cacti and succulents is the most effective approach to preventing diseases. Regularly monitor your plants, provide proper care, and maintain good sanitation practices to ensure their well-being.

Management of Common Challenges

Environmental Challenges

Temperature Extremes: Cacti and succulents are adapted to various temperature ranges, but extreme heat or cold can stress the plants. Frost and freezing temperatures, particularly, can damage some species, leading to tissue damage and discoloration.

Inadequate Lighting: Insufficient sunlight can result in elongated and weak growth. On the other hand, too much direct sunlight can cause sunburn and damage to the plant's tissues.

Humidity Fluctuations: Fluctuations in humidity levels can stress cacti and succulents, especially those that prefer dry conditions. High humidity can increase the risk of fungal diseases, while low humidity can lead to dehydration and wilting.

Poor Air Circulation: Inadequate air circulation can increase plants' humidity and make them more susceptible to diseases like powdery mildew and fungal infections.

Overwatering and Underwatering

Overwatering: One of the most common mistakes in succulent care is overwatering. Cacti and succulents are adapted to survive in arid conditions and prefer infrequent, deep watering. Overwatering can lead to root rot and other fungal diseases.

Underwatering: Underwatering can cause cacti and succulents to become dehydrated and may result in wilting, shriveling, or the appearance of dry, crispy leaves.

Nutritional Deficiencies

Nitrogen, Phosphorus, or Potassium Deficiencies: Like all plants, cacti and succulents require essential nutrients for healthy growth. A lack of nitrogen, phosphorus, or potassium can lead to stunted growth, yellowing leaves, and poor overall health.

Plant Stress

Physical Damage: Accidental damage to the plant's stem, roots, or leaves can create openings for pathogens to enter and cause infections. Avoid rough handling or contact with sharp objects.

Transplant Shock: Transplanting cacti and succulents can cause stress, particularly if the roots are disturbed. Transplant shock may result in wilting, discoloration, or slower growth as the plant adjusts to its new environment.

Environmental Stressors: Exposure to extreme weather conditions, such as strong winds, intense sunlight, or sudden temperature changes, can stress cacti and succulents, affecting their overall health and appearance.

To effectively address these challenges:

- Know your plant's specific requirements and adapt care practices accordingly.
- Provide the right light, water, and humidity for the specific species.
- Monitor your plants regularly for signs of stress, pests, and diseases.

- Take preventive measures to protect your plants from extreme environmental conditions.
- Address any issues promptly to prevent further damage or the spread of problems.

By understanding and addressing these challenges, you can create a suitable and supportive environment for your cacti and succulents, promoting their optimal health and ensuring their longevity in your care.

Chapter 9: Companion Planting with Cacti and Succulents

Companion planting is an excellent gardening concept where cacti and succulents are grown with other compatible plant species to maximize the garden's health. Just like the concept of symbiosis, companion planting is based on the idea that certain plant species, when grown together, will enhance growth, prevent pests, and promote nutrient uptake. This technique has been used since ancient times and is categorized as one of the most sustainable approaches to gardening.

A harmonious garden can be created by planting companion plants that support each other's growth and well-being. Some plants can produce pest-mitigating chemicals, whereas others can benefit from nitrogen fixation in the soil.

Companion planting is an excellent gardening concept where cacti and succulents are grown with other compatible plant species to maximize the garden's health.

https://www.pexels.com/photo/potted-flowers-placed-in-cozy-room-4813268/

Although companion planting has numerous benefits, it's necessary to understand that each plant has specific requirements. Not every plant combination will work or be mutually beneficial. Therefore, studying plant species and doing your research before implementing companion planting techniques is crucial. Still, companion planting is an excellent way for gardeners to enhance biodiversity, reduce dependence on pesticides and fertilizers, and make the plants resilient. When done right, this symbiotic companionship of plants can go a long way toward reducing costs for pesticides and other problems in your garden.

The Purpose of Companion Planting

Although cacti and succulents can withstand harsh conditions and don't need intensive maintenance, companion planting can still serve several purposes. Companion planting fosters a sustainable and holistic approach to gardening as it can naturally prevent the spread of pests and diseases.

Pest Control

Aromatic herbs like rosemary, lavender, and thyme can be planted alongside cacti, deterring harmful insects and pests. Planting these companion plants creates a pest-free ecosystem that reduces the need for chemical pesticides.

Biodiversity

Planting compatible species with your cacti and succulents promotes biodiversity. Several companion plants can also attract beneficial insects, pollinators, and other microorganisms that can nurture the garden's overall health. For example, flowering companion plants can enhance pollination rates in other plants by attracting butterflies.

Soil Health

Companion plants like legumes and beans encourage the development of nitrogen-fixing bacteria, which enrich the soil with nitrogen. Cacti and succulents benefit from the nitrogen reserves in the soil, decreasing the dependency on chemical fertilizers. Improved soil fertility will eventually promote healthier growth.

Visual Appeal

Adding visual interest and diversity to your cacti is also an added benefit of companion gardening. You can choose from a wide range of plants, herbs, and other ornamental plant species to make an aesthetically pleasing and harmonious display.

Microclimate Modification

Although cacti can tolerate drought-like conditions and high temperatures, the intense summer heat can affect their health. Planting companion plants that can provide shade to the cacti during the intense summer heat creates better growing conditions and lets you create microclimate conditions.

Natural Pest Predators

Several companion plants attract ladybugs, plant-friendly beetles, and lace wigs, which feed on common pests. These natural pest predators can minimize the dependency on insecticides or chemical interventions.

Improved Pollination

If you have a full-size garden, choosing plants like the African daisy, Mexican daisy, fortnight lily, red valerian, etc., with your cacti will increase pollination, keeping the garden thriving. Marigolds and sunflowers can also be used in specific areas to promote pollination.

Weed Suppression

Companion plants like mint, artemisia, catmint, and stonecrop prevent weeds. These plants don't leave enough space for the root systems of weeds to take root and thrive. Dense plantings can physically shade the soil in extremely hot environments, further preventing weeds from taking hold.

Space Optimization

You can easily elevate the garden's aesthetics and use every nook and cranny by planting visually striking plants. For example, growing a tall or climbing plant with cacti is an excellent choice if you have limited space. The tall, rising plants will provide your cacti enough shade, protecting them from direct sunlight. Similarly, virtually any available space can be used accordingly, creating a biodiverse ecosystem.

Having tons of benefits, companion planting can pave the way toward sustainable gardening, keeping the plants healthy and robust. Imagine creating a garden of cacti and succulents, surrounded by magnificent flowering companion plants that can attract plant-friendly insects, herbs, and aromatic plants to ward off pests and plants like alfalfa and clovers, keeping the soil rich in nitrogen. All these benefits are possible through companion planting. However, it will need research and knowledge about companion plants compatible with cacti and succulents.

Suitable Companion Plants

Selecting suitable plants involves considering their compatibility regarding growth habits, nutrient needs, pest management, and mutual benefits. Here are some examples of compatible companion plants and the reasons for pairing them:

Selecting suitable plants involves considering their compatibility regarding growth habits, nutrient needs, pest management, and mutual benefits.

https://pixabay.com/photos/chilli-lavender-red-mauve-orange-265756/

Succulents

Agaves, sedums, and echeverias are some succulent companion plants for cacti. Succulents and cacti have virtually similar growth requirements, making them ideal plants. Their sunlight, soil, and nutrient requirements are the same. When planted together, Cacti and succulents create a visually striking and cohesive desert landscape. Veteran cacti gardeners recommend planting succulents near cacti, adding color, texture, and depth to the landscape.

Creeping Plants

For lush foliage, consider low-growing and spreading plants like creeping thyme, ice plants, and various sedum species to add to your garden. These plants can provide excellent soil cover around the cacti, serving as a natural mulch that retains moisture, regulates temperature, and prevents weed growth. They also create a living carpet that adds visual interest and complements the upright forms of cacti. These creeping plants can also provide a feasible habitat for plant-friendly insects and pests, limiting harmful pest infestation.

Wildflowers

Desert-adapted wildflowers like desert marigolds (Baileya multiradiata), desert bluebells (Phacelia campanularia), and globe mallow (Sphaeralcea spp.) can bring bursts of vibrant color to your cactus garden. These flowers attract pollinators, such as bees and butterflies, which help improve pollination for cacti and wildflowers.

Aloe Vera

Aloe vera is not only a popular companion plant for cacti due to its similar water requirements but also because of its practical uses. Aloe vera's succulent leaves contain a soothing gel that can be used for various skin ailments, making it a functional addition to your garden. Planting aloe vera near cacti provides some shade and protection to the cacti while offering a source of natural skincare.

Lavender

Lavender has such a pleasant fragrance and can also attract beneficial insects. Planting lavender near cacti can create a sensory experience in your garden and support pollinators like bees. The tall, slender stems and purple blooms of lavender contrast beautifully with the spiky, textured appearance of cacti.

Yucca

Yucca plants share a similar arid habitat with cacti and can make excellent companions in a desert-themed garden. Their upright growth habit and dramatic flower spikes add visual interest and height to the landscape. Yuccas can create a striking backdrop for cacti while contributing to the overall desert aesthetic.

Herbs

Certain herbs that thrive in dry conditions, such as rosemary, sage, and oregano, can be planted alongside cacti. These herbs add aromatic scents to your garden and also serve culinary and medicinal purposes. Their drought-tolerant nature and compatibility with cacti make them versatile companions.

Rocks and Gravel

Incorporating decorative rocks and gravel into your cactus garden can mimic the natural desert environment and also have practical benefits. Rocks and gravel help regulate soil temperature, prevent erosion, and enhance drainage. They also create a visually appealing hardscape that complements the unique textures of cacti.

When planning your companion planting arrangement, consider the specific needs of each plant, including water, sunlight, soil, and space requirements. Group plants with similar needs together to ensure they thrive and harmonize. Regular monitoring, proper spacing, and adjusting care routines as needed will contribute to a successful and visually captivating cactus garden with well-chosen companion plants.

Checking Plant Compatibility

Considering compatibility in terms of light requirements, water needs, growth habits, and soil preferences is essential to create a successful and harmonious garden environment. Each plant species has unique characteristics and preferences, and understanding these factors helps gardeners make informed decisions about plant placement and combinations. Here's why compatibility matters:

Light Requirements

Different plants have varying light preferences, ranging from full sun to partial shade or full shade. Planting species with similar light requirements together ensures that all plants get the appropriate amount of sunlight. Placing shade-loving plants in direct sunlight or sun-loving plants in the shade can lead to stress, wilting, or poor growth. By grouping plants with similar light needs, you optimize their overall health and vitality.

Water Needs

Water requirements can vary widely among plant species. Some plants are drought-tolerant and prefer infrequent watering, while others need consistently moist soil. Pairing plants with similar water needs ensures that all plants receive the appropriate amount of water, preventing overwatering or underwatering. Overwatering leads to root rot and other water-related issues, while underwatering can cause plants to wilt and weaken.

Growth Habits

Different plants have different growth patterns, such as height, spread, and growth speed. Managing the growth habitat is essential to prevent overcrowded plants and make the existing plants fight for resources. For example, if you pair a fast-growing plant with cacti or succulents, the aggressive-growing plant can easily outcompete nearby plants, using up all the soil resources themselves. Selecting plants with complementary growth habits ensures that all plants have sufficient space to develop fully without restricting one another's growth.

Soil Preferences

Each plant has varying soil preferences, which include different pH levels and nutrient requirements. Soil humidity and soil texture. Some plants prefer well-draining soil, whereas others prefer thriving in moist and loamy soil. Placing plants with similar soil preferences together helps create an ideal growing environment for each species. Additionally, certain plants can improve soil conditions for others through nitrogen fixation or soil aeration.

Plant Compatibility

Choose plants with similar growing requirements regarding sunlight, water, and soil preferences. Avoid pairing plants with wildly different needs, which can lead to resource competition and hinder their growth. For example, pair sun-loving or shade-tolerant plants together to ensure they flourish in their respective environments.

Growth Habits

Another issue to think about is the growth habits of the plants and how they will interact physically in the garden. Tall plants can provide shade or support for shorter plants. For instance, tall sunflowers can offer shade to cacti succulents. Lower-growing lettuces or provide a sturdy trellis for climbing beans.

Nutrient Needs

Pair plants with different nutrient needs together to ensure efficient use of soil resources. Some plants, like legumes, fix nitrogen in the soil, benefiting nearby plants that require nitrogen for healthy growth. For example, grow nitrogen-fixing beans or peas alongside growing succulents and cacti to provide them with the required nitrogen to thrive.

Pest-Repelling Properties

Use companion plants that deter pests or attract beneficial insects. Certain herbs, flowers, or aromatic plants have natural pest-repelling properties, which can help protect nearby susceptible crops. For example, planting marigolds can repel pests and insects, preventing infestations that could potentially affect the cacti.

Attracting Pollinators

Include plants that attract pollinators like bees, butterflies, and other beneficial insects. Flowers with abundant nectar and pollen can increase pollination rates and fruiting. For instance, planting lavender or borage near cacti will increase their pollination rate.

Succession Planting

Pair plants with different growing seasons or maturity rates to keep the surroundings in control. For example, you can plant fast-growing crops like radishes or lettuce alongside succulents when you need to provide shade, limit soil erosion, and keep weed production at bay. These faster crops are harvested, allowing more space and resources for the slower ones to expand.

Aesthetic Appeal

Consider the visual impact of companion plant combinations. Combine plants with contrasting colors, textures, and heights to create visually appealing and harmonious garden displays. For example, pairing purple basil and bright yellow marigolds with cacti and succulents can create a striking and vibrant color contrast.

Native and Regional Plant Choices

Select native or regionally adapted plants for companion planting to support local ecosystems and encourage beneficial wildlife, such as native pollinators. Native plants are often well-suited to the local climate and require less maintenance.

In summary, pairing suitable companion plants with your cacti and succulents involves thoughtful planning, taking into account plant compatibility, nutrient needs, growth habits, pest-repelling properties, and aesthetics. By creating a diverse and balanced garden ecosystem, gardeners can maximize productivity, reduce pest pressures, support pollinators, and enhance the overall health and beauty of their gardens.

By considering these compatibility factors, gardeners reap several benefits:

Efficient Resource Allocation: Pairing plants with similar requirements will minimize the waste of resources. Water and fertilizer can be applied more precisely, ensuring that each plant gets what it needs without excess or deficiency.

Reduced Maintenance Efforts: When plants are compatible, they are more likely to thrive in their environment, leading to fewer pest problems and less plant stress. This can reduce the need for intervention and maintenance efforts.

Aesthetically Pleasing Arrangements: Grouping plants with complementary growth habits, colors, and textures can create visually appealing landscapes or garden beds.

Enhanced Biodiversity: By selecting a diverse range of compatible plants, gardeners promote biodiversity and attract a wider array of beneficial insects and wildlife to the garden.

Overall, considering compatibility in terms of light, water, growth habits, and soil preferences is crucial for successful gardening. It enables gardeners to create balanced, sustainable, and visually pleasing garden environments where each plant thrives and contributes to the overall health and productivity of the space.

Companion Plant Recommendations

Pest-Repelling Companion Plants

Pest-repelling companion plants emit natural compounds or scents that deter common garden pests. Including these plants in your garden can help reduce pest populations and minimize the need for chemical pesticides. Some examples of pest-repelling companion plants are:

Marigolds: Marigolds are well-known for repelling aphids, whiteflies, and nematodes. Their distinct scent acts as a natural deterrent, making them effective companions for vegetables like tomatoes, peppers, and potatoes.

Nasturtiums: Nasturtiums are another excellent choice for pest control. They deter aphids, whiteflies, squash bugs, and cucumber beetles. Planting nasturtiums near cucumbers, squash, and tomatoes can help protect these vulnerable crops from common garden pests.

Nitrogen-Fixing Plants and Soil Enhancement

Nitrogen-fixing plants improve soil fertility by enriching it with nitrogen, an essential nutrient for plant growth. These plants have a symbiotic relationship with nitrogen-fixing bacteria, which convert atmospheric nitrogen into a form that is readily available to plants. Examples of nitrogen-fixing plants include:

Legumes (Beans, Peas, Lentils, etc.) are well-known nitrogen-fixers. They form nodules on their roots, where nitrogen-fixing bacteria reside. As these plants grow, they take nitrogen from the air and store it in the soil, benefiting neighboring plants like leafy greens, brassicas, and corn.

Pollinator Attractants

Pollinator-attracting companion plants play a vital role in garden ecosystems by attracting bees, butterflies, and other beneficial insects. These pollinators are essential for fruit set in many flowering plants. Examples of pollinator-attracting companion plants include:

Bee-Friendly Flowers: Flowers like zinnias, sunflowers, cosmos, and lavender are attractive to bees and other pollinators. Planting these flowers near fruiting plants like cucumbers, tomatoes, strawberries, and melons can enhance pollination rates and increase the yield of these crops.

Aesthetic Combinations

Aesthetic combinations focus on creating visually appealing garden displays by combining plants with contrasting colors, textures, and forms. Some examples of aesthetic combinations are:

Color and Texture Contrasts: Pairing plants with contrasting colors and textures can create striking visual displays. For instance, you can plant purple sage with yellow marigolds for a complementary color combination or red roses with white daisies for a classic contrast.

Container Gardening and Indoor Companions

Companion planting is not limited to traditional outdoor gardens. It can also be used in container gardening and indoor plant arrangements.

Some examples of container and indoor companionship are:

Herbs and Vegetables: Planting herbs like basil, mint, or parsley alongside compact vegetables in containers can save space and provide fresh herbs for culinary use. For example, pairing cherry tomatoes with basil or salad greens with chives can be a practical and aesthetically pleasing combination.

Succulents and Cacti: Mixing different varieties of succulents and cacti in containers can create beautiful, low-maintenance displays for indoor and outdoor spaces. Combining these resilient plants' different shapes, colors, and sizes can result in eye-catching arrangements.

Care and Maintenance Considerations

While planning companion plantings, it's essential to consider each plant's specific care and maintenance needs. Some key considerations include:

Watering: Group plants with similar water needs together to ensure efficient watering and prevent over or under-watering. For example, pairing drought-tolerant plants like succulents with other low-water-need plants can simplify watering routines.

Pruning: Plan for growth habits and space requirements to avoid overcrowding and provide enough room for plants to grow without shading each other excessively. Regular pruning and trimming of plants help maintain the desired balance in the garden.

Pest Management: Consider the pest-repelling properties of companion plants when planning your garden layout. Including pest-repelling plants strategically throughout the garden can help naturally deter common pests, reducing the need for chemical pesticides.

By considering these factors and carefully selecting companion plants based on their benefits and compatibility, gardeners can create thriving and sustainable garden environments. Companion planting fosters biodiversity, enhances natural pest control, and adds aesthetic appeal to the garden, ultimately contributing to a more balanced and harmonious ecosystem.

Appendix: A-Z of Cacti and Succulents: Species Identification Reference

With thousands of species of cacti around the globe, there is at least one succulent for every letter of the alphabet. This appendix is an A-Z guide to some of the most interesting and easily identifiable cacti and succulents you might come across.

Acanthocalycium Glaucum

Scientific Name: Acanthocalycium Glaucum

Common Name: Acanthocalycium Glaucum

This takes a circular shape and often elongates into a single cactus. The stem grows up to 5.9 inches tall and around 3.15 inches in diameter. The Acanthocalycium Glaucum has 8 to 14 ribs, which are all covered by pruina for protection. The plant's spines are around 0.9 long and are clear at the base and dark at the ends. The Acanthocalycium Glaucum also has no central spine. It grows either red or yellow flowers that grow up to 1o inches tall.

Acanthocalycium Thionanthum

Scientific Name: Acanthocalycium Thionanthum

Common Name: Acanthocalycium Thionanthum

This cactus has a single habit that may branch out slowly as it grows older. It grows up to 4.7 inches long and 3.9 inches in diameter. The plant's stem is globular and is light green to bluish green and has 9 to 15 ribs. Younger cacti have black spines that turn yellowish as they age. The spines are long and sharp and are found in groups of 5 to 10 in each areola, along with one to four central spines. The Acanthocalycium Thionanthum grows bell-shaped bright yellow flowers and rarely grows orange or white ones.

Ball Cactus

Scientific Name: Parodia Magnifica

Common Name: Ball Cactus

This cactus has a ball-shaped to cylinder-like stem that grows up to 12 inches tall and 18 inches wide. The cacti of this variety can grow in clusters and frequently produce yellow, pink, red, or orange flowers. Younger cacti have white spikes that become yellowish-brown as they age.

Cabega

Scientific Name: Austrocephalocereus dybowskii

Common Name: Cabega

Cabegas are 3.9 inches in diameter and have cylinder-like stems. They grow in groups and are covered in white fluff. Each stem has around 20 ribs and two to three central spines, along with numerous tiny radial spines. Cabega flowers are white and bell-shaped.

Dutchman's Pipe Cactus

Scientific Name: Epiphyllum oxypetalum

Common Name: Dutchman's Pipe Cactus

This cactus can grow over 9.8 feet long and has several branches. The stems can grow anywhere between 6.5 to a whopping 19.6 feet long, causing them to flatten and lie sideways. They grow ample large white flowers and rarely produce fruit.

Echinopsis

Scientific Name: Echinopsis Thelegona

Common Name: Echinopsis

This cactus grows up to 7.2 feet tall and 3.9 inches in diameter. It produces a few shoots, and the stem has 12 to 13 ribs. Echnoposis is characterized by its areoles, which grow in hexagon-like patterns. The cactus has five to eight radial spines and one middle spine. In rare cases, Echiposis can exist with two middle spines. The plant grows white flowers that are around 8.6 inches long and 6.6 inches in diameter.

Fairy Castle

Scientific Name: Acanthocereus Tetragonus

Common Name: Fairy Castle

The Acanthocereus Tetragonus is among the easiest cacti to spot because it resembles a castle that a fairy would live in. The Fairy Castle has several stems, each of a different height. The average height of the stems is 3.2 feet. The stems have white spines along their ribs and grow at least a hundred branches and branchlets.

Giant Chin Cactus

Scientific Name: Gymnocalycium Saglionis

Common Name: Giant Chin Cactus

The Giant Chin Cactus is a single, huge stem with long spines. The stem looks like a somewhat flat sphere and is 7.4 to 15.7 inches in diameter. Most of the Giant Chin Cacti are 5.9 to 11.8 inches tall. However, they can grow up to 2.9 feet tall. They have one to three straight central spines and 10 to 15 curved radial ones. They produce red, globular fruits and funnelform blooms.

Hooker's Orchid Cactus

Scientific Name: Epiphyllum hookeri

Common Name: Hooker's Orchid Cactus

You could mistake the Epiphyllum Hookeri for a non-succulent at first glance because of its long foliage. However, if you look closely enough, you'll see the stems and spines of the cactus. The plant produces beautiful white flowers and grows up to 9 inches tall.

Johnson's Beehive Cactus

Scientific Name: Echinomastus Johnsonii

Common Name: Johnson's Beehive Cactus

This cactus has cylinder-like stems that grow up to 10 inches tall and 4 inches in diameter. It has countless bent spines that come in various colors, like purple, red, yellow, pink, and gray. Johnson's Beehive Cactus produces pink and yellow flowers that grow a little over 3 inches tall.

Koko

Scientific Name: Echinopsis Formosa

Common Name: Koko

Koko cacti are either globular stems with golden yellow spines that grow in clusters or cylindrical-shaped stems with creamy white spines that grow alone. Echinopsis Formosa grows up to 28 inches tall and 16 inches in diameter. They aren't quick to grow, so it will take them at least three decades to reach their full growth potential. Koko cacti grow yellow flowers.

Lady Finger Cactus

Scientific Name: Mammillaria Elongata

Common Name: Lady Finger Cactus

These cactus stems take the shape of fingers, with each growing up to 8 inches tall and 1.2 inches wide. Their spines are golden yellow, contrasting perfectly against the dark green stems. The cactus blooms with light pink, yellow, or white flowers.

Mammillaria Dixanthocentron

Scientific Name: Mammillaria Dixanthocentron

Common Name: Mammillaria Dixanthocentron

This cylindrical cactus has two to four yellow and soft reddish central spines and 19 to 20 white radial ones. It grows up to 11.8 inches tall and is 2.7 to 3.14 inches in diameter. It produces small, light red or pink flowers that are around 3.9 inches long. It also produces yellow or orange fruit.

Old Lady Cactus

Scientific Name: Mammillaria Hahniana

Common Name: Old Lady Cactus

This cactus is a natural work of art. It has a globular stem and often grows in clusters. The average single stem is 4 inches tall and 5 inches in diameter but can reach 10 inches in height over time. While the spikey fuzz ball looks interesting on its own, the violet-red flowers that blossom during summer create an astonishing crown-like effect.

Rattail Cactus

Scientific Name: Aporocactus Flagelliformis

Common Name: Rattail Cactus

This is yet another succulent that you can easily identify. It is characterized by its long, thin, snake-like stems, which grow up to 4 feet tall. The Rattail Cactus produces captivating purplish-red flowers but may sometimes bloom orange and pink ones.

Saguaro

Scientific Name: Carnegiea gigantea

Common Name: Saguaro

This giant succulent is what comes to most people's minds when they hear the word "cactus." It is how this plant is depicted in most cartoons and movies that are set in the Mexican or Arizona deserts. The cactus grows up to a staggering 50 feet in length and 30 inches in diameter. Some cacti grow one to five arm-like branches, while others grow none at all.

Thimble Cactus

Scientific Name: Mammillaria Gracilis

Common Name: Thimble Cactus

Many people prefer to keep Thimble Cacti as home plants due to their unique and decorative appearance and small size. They grow in clusters, with each growing up to 3 inches tall and 2 inches wide. Thimble Cacti produce white or pink flowers as well.

Zebra Plant

Scientific Name: Haworthia Fasciata

Common Name: Zebra Plant

This eye-catching succulent is easy to identify from miles away. It has glossy, long, and pointy dark green leaves, with creamy white stripes highlighting the veins, resembling zebra skin. The succulent produces yellow or white flowers at the top of the stem.

Conclusion

It's time to refresh your memory with a brief summary. In the biological sense, a cactus is a succulent, but gardeners and horticulturists define them as two different plants. Succulents have been evolving for millions of years, but they became a trend among humans soon after the birth of social media.

There are over 10,000 species of succulents, of which 1700 are cacti. So, it may be difficult for you to choose just one for your collection. Simply remember four important points: growing conditions, plant preferences, available resources, and the ultimate goal for the plant.

After selecting the right species, be very careful with the planting process. Plant two or more succulents as far apart as possible and prepare the planting area with suitable soil and allowance for drainage. If you follow all the best techniques, then there is a high chance that your plant will grow into the perfect specimen your heart desires. Also, since cacti and succulents are mostly ornamental, don't forget to arrange them in a visually appealing manner.

Then comes the most important part of nurturing these plants: watering, or rather, the lack of it. You need to take great care that you don't overwater any species of cacti or succulents. Use the right watering tools and techniques, take the temperature of the surroundings into account, and make sure to assess the moisture level in the soil before pouring in more water.

That said, it is absurdly simple to care for and maintain your cacti and succulents since they rarely ever need anything. You just need to remember a few significant points, like fertilizing options, seasonal care adjustments, pest and disease control, and essential care practices.

Furthermore, since cacti and succulents are primarily ornamental, you can prune them into appealing shapes and figures. While it's not as easy as pruning a bonsai tree since its leaves and stems are considerably thicker, it's not an exhausting process either. Pruning and cutting these plants has a side benefit, too. You can use the chopped parts to grow more plants of the same kind with a technique called propagation or cloning.

Multiplying and expanding your garden is an intriguing prospect, but you need to make sure that you have planted all the necessary companion plants. They not only beautify your backyard but also help in the growth of other plants.

It is recommended that you keep this book open at all times throughout the planting process to refer back to specific instructions, at least during your first few tries. Once you have retained all the information shown here and you have become used to the entire procedure, you can let go of the crutches and soar high and free into the realm of cacti and succulents, all on your own.

Here's another book by Dion Rosser that you might like

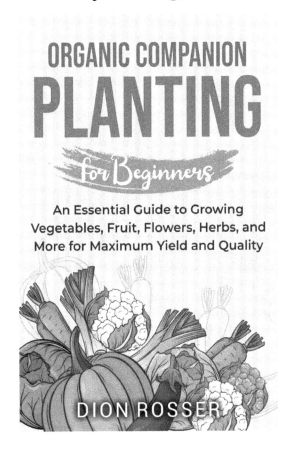

ORGANIC COMPANION
PLANTING
for Beginners

An Essential Guide to Growing
Vegetables, Fruit, Flowers, Herbs, and
More for Maximum Yield and Quality

DION ROSSER

References

(N.d.). Businesscasestudies.co.uk. https://businesscasestudies.co.uk/amazing-history-of-succulents-where-do-they-come-from/

(N.d.). Gardenia.net. https://www.gardenia.net/guide/great-shrubs-as-companion-plants-for-your-succulents

(N.d.). Weekand.com. https://www.weekand.com/home-garden/article/pollinate-cactus-18060952.php

(N.d.-a). Masterclass.com. https://www.masterclass.com/articles/bunny-ear-cactus-guide#:~:text=The%20bunny%20ear%20cactus%20is,or%20in%20outdoor%20rock%20gardens.

(N.d.-b). Masterclass.com. https://www.masterclass.com/articles/bunny-ear-cactus-guide#:~:text=In%20order%20to%20keep%20your,moisture%20and%20drain%20excess%20water.

(N.d.-c). Gardenia.net. https://www.gardenia.net/plant/epiphyllum-oxypetalum#:~:text=Water%20regularly%20during%20the%20growing,damage%20or%20kill%20the%20plant.

(N.d.-d). A-z-animals.com. https://a-z-animals.com/plants/old-lady-cactus/#:~:text=This%20plant%20thrives%20outside%20in,inside%20during%20winter%20and%20fall

14 fragrant succulents & cacti (you will love). (2022, February 19). AskGardening. https://askgardening.com/fragrant-succulents-cactus/

25 beautiful cactus garden ideas. (n.d.). Trees.com. https://www.trees.com/gardening-and-landscaping/cactus-garden-ideas

29 types of cactus (with pictures and names) – identification guide. (2021, October 11). Leafy Place. https://leafyplace.com/types-of-cacti/

Abramson, A., & Milbrand, L. (2022, April 14). How to propagate succulents from leaves or stems. Real Simple. https://www.realsimple.com/home-organizing/gardening/indoor/how-to-propagate-succulents

Acanthocalycium glaucum. (n.d.). https://www.cactus-art.biz/schede/ACANTHOCALYCIUM/Acanthocalycium_glaucum/Acanthocalycium_glaucum/Acanthocalycium_glaucum.htm

Acanthocereus tetragonus cv. Fairytale castle. (n.d.). http://www.llifle.com/Encyclopedia/CACTI/Family/Cactaceae/6981/Acanthocereus_tetragonus_cv._Fairytale_castle

Apples and pears: espalier pruning and training / RHS Gardening. (n.d.). Org.uk. https://www.rhs.org.uk/fruit/apples/training-espalier

Baldwin, D. L. (2020, February 12). How succulents combat global warming. Debra Lee Baldwin. https://debraleebaldwin.com/succulent-plants/succulents-combat-global-warming/

Baldwin, D. L. (2021, March 11). What makes succulents SUCCULENT? Debra Lee Baldwin. https://debraleebaldwin.com/cactus/science-of-succulence/

Balogh, A. (2017, May 17). How to plant succulents + 8 growing tips – garden design. Gardendesign.com; Garden Design Magazine. https://www.gardendesign.com/succulents/planting.html

Beaulieu, D. (2013, January 20). What's the difference between Cacti and succulents? The Spruce. https://www.thespruce.com/difference-between-cacti-and-succulents-3976741

Blumberg, P. O. (2020, June 16). 5 expert tips to take care of your cacti. Southern Living. https://www.southernliving.com/garden/plants/cactus-care-tips

Blumberg, P. O. (2020, June 16). 5 expert tips to take care of your cacti. Southern Living. https://www.southernliving.com/garden/plants/cactus-care-tips

Boeckmann, C. (n.d.). Aloe Vera. Almanac.com. https://www.almanac.com/plant/aloe-vera

Box, S. (n.d.). Common Pests & Diseases Treatment for Succulents. Succulents Box. https://succulentsbox.com/pages/common-pests-diseases

Box, S. (n.d.). How to care for your cactus and succulent arrangements. Succulents Box. https://succulentsbox.com/blogs/blog/how-to-plant-cacti-and-succulents-together

Brazilian prickly pear (Brasiliopuntia brasiliensis) Flower, Leaf, Care, Uses. (n.d.). PictureThis. https://www.picturethisai.com/wiki/Brasiliopuntia_brasiliensis.html

Brazilian prickly pear Care (Watering, Fertilize, Pruning, Propagation). (n.d.). PictureThis. https://www.picturethisai.com/care/Brasiliopuntia_brasiliensis.html

Brown, D. L. (n.d.). Cacti and succulents. Umn.edu. https://extension.umn.edu/houseplants/cacti-and-succulents

Brown, D. L. (n.d.). Cacti and succulents. Umn.edu. https://extension.umn.edu/houseplants/cacti-and-succulents

Brown, D. L. (n.d.). Cacti and succulents. Umn.edu. https://extension.umn.edu/houseplants/cacti-and-succulents

Bunny Ears Cactus. (n.d.). Planterina. https://planterina.com/blogs/indoor-plant-care/bunny-ears-cactus

Burro's tail, Sedum morganianum. (n.d.). Wisconsin Horticulture. https://hort.extension.wisc.edu/articles/burros-tail-sedum-morganianum/

Cacti and succulent problems. (2019, March 1). About The Garden Magazine. https://www.aboutthegarden.com.au/cacti-and-succulent-problems/

Cactus care & tips. (2022, March 13). Smith Rock Cactus Company. https://smithrockcactuscompany.com/cactus-care-tips/

Cactus care & tips. (2022, March 13). Smith Rock Cactus Company. https://smithrockcactuscompany.com/cactus-care-tips/

Cactus care. (2007, August 15). HowStuffWorks. https://home.howstuffworks.com/cactus-care1.htm

Cactus care: How to water cacti (cactuses)? (2018, August 31). Terrarium Planting Guide. https://plantinterrarium.com/cactus-care-how-to-water-cacti-cactuses/

Cactus corner project – history. (n.d.). Theinkrag.com. https://www.theinkrag.com/cactus_corner_project/historycc.html

Cactus. (n.d.). Mcgill.Ca

Carberry, A. (2005, January 29). How to grow a Cactus. WikiHow. https://www.wikihow.com/Grow-a-Cactus

Caring for Cacti & succulents – indoor plants – Westland. (2018, February 5). Garden Health. https://www.gardenhealth.com/advice/plants-flowers/how-to-care-for-cacti-and-succulents

Caring for Cacti & succulents – indoor plants – Westland. (2018, February 5). Garden Health. https://www.gardenhealth.com/advice/plants-flowers/how-to-care-for-cacti-and-succulents

Carnegiea gigantea | Landscape Plants | Oregon State University. (n.d.). https://landscapeplants.oregonstate.edu/plants/carnegiea-gigantea

Common Succulent diseases and pests to look out for. (n.d.). Plants For All Seasons. https://www.plantsforallseasons.co.uk/blogs/succulent-care/common-succulent-diseases-and-pests-to-look-out-for

Cooperative extension: Garden and yard. (2011, December 2). Cooperative Extension: Garden and Yard. https://extension.umaine.edu/gardening/manual/propagation/plant-propagation/

Cowen, J. (2021, May 2). 5 best succulent and cactus fertilizer + how to fertilize. The Yard and Garden. https://theyardandgarden.com/best-succulent-and-cactus-fertilizer/

Cox, M. (n.d.). How to prune topiary. Saga.co.uk. https://www.saga.co.uk/magazine/home-garden/gardening/advice-tips/pruning/how-to-prune-topiary

Creative Wilder. (2021, February 26). 4 benefits of propagating plants. Pop Wilder Website. https://www.popwilder.com/post/4-benefits-of-propagating-plants

D, J. (2023). 132 Different Types of Cacti listed in A to Z Photo Database. Home Stratosphere. https://www.homestratosphere.com/types-of-cacti/?fwp_paged=5

Edinburg Scenic Wetlands, & World Birding Center. (n.d.). Cochineal insect: The natural dye. Edinburg Scenic Wetlands and World Birding Center. https://edinburgwbc.org/news/f/cochineal-insect-the-natural-dye

Eg. (2021). Trichocereus thelegonus / Echinopsis thelegona Friedrich & Rowley. Trichocereus.net – Cactus Seeds and Books! https://trichocereus.net/trichocereus-thelegonus-echinopsis-thelegona-friedrich-rowley/

Epiphyllum oxypetalum. (n.d.). http://www.llifle.com/Encyclopedia/CACTI/Family/Cactaceae/8223/Epiphyllum_oxypetalum

Espiritu, K. (2019, November 6). How to grow a ponytail palm outdoors. Epic Gardening. https://www.epicgardening.com/growing-ponytail-palm-outdoors/

Forbes, N. (2022, July 15). Growing cacti & succulents indoors. Dennis' 7 Dees | Landscaping Services & Garden Centers; Dennis' 7 Dees Landscaping & Garden Centers. https://dennis7dees.com/growing-cacti-succulents-indoors/

Foster, N. (2022, May 21). Indoor cactus care for beginners (2023 guide). Joy Us Garden | Care, Propagation, and Pruning; Joy Us Garden. https://www.joyusgarden.com/indoor-cactus-care/

Full guide on cactus diseases, pests and treatments. (2018, October 26). Terrarium Planting Guide. https://plantinterrarium.com/full-guide-on-cactus-diseases-pests-and-treatments/

García, A. (2022, October 24). The importance of Nopal cactus to Mexicans. Mansion Mauresque. https://mansionmauresque.com/the-importance-of-nopal-cactus-to-mexicans/

Gaumond, A. (2023, July 31). The cactus: A guide to its meaning, symbolism & cultural significance. Petal Republic. https://www.petalrepublic.com/cactus-meaning/

Gilmer, M. (2015, January 16). The Desert Sun. The Desert Sun. https://www.desertsun.com/story/life/home-garden/maureen-gilmer/2015/01/16/san-pedro-cactus-ornamental-maureen-gilmer/21789499/

Gotter, A. (2017, May 25). Nopal cactus: Benefits, uses, and more. Healthline. https://www.healthline.com/health/nopal

Grant, B. L. (2012, December 30). Starfish flower cactus: Tips for growing starfish flowers indoors. Gardening Know How. https://www.gardeningknowhow.com/ornamental/cacti-succulents/starfish-flower/growing-starfish-flowers.htm

Grant, B. L. (2014, September 12). Established plants are tall and leggy: What to do for leggy plant growth. Gardening Know How. https://www.gardeningknowhow.com/plant-problems/environmental/established-plants-leggy.htm

Grant, B. L. (2018, May 19). Walking stick cholla info: Tips on caring for walking stick chollas. Gardening Know How. https://www.gardeningknowhow.com/ornamental/cacti-succulents/cholla-cactus/caring-for-walking-stick-chollas.htm

Gregarious Inc. (n.d.-a). Old Man Cactus. Greg.App. https://greg.app/plant-care/old-man-cactus-cephalocereus-senilis

Gregarious Inc. (n.d.-b). What Soil is Best for a Christmas Cactus? Greg.App. https://greg.app/blog/cactus/what-soil-is-best-for-a-christmas-cactus/

Growing aloe. (n.d.). Miraclegro.com. https://miraclegro.com/en-us/indoor-gardening/growing-aloe.html

Gymnocalycium saglionis subs. tilcarense. (n.d.). http://www.llifle.com/Encyclopedia/CACTI/Family/Cactaceae/12119/Gymnocalycium_saglionis_subs._tilcarense

Hailey, L. (2022, June 22). 15 companion planting mistakes to avoid this season. All About Gardening. https://www.allaboutgardening.com/companion-planting-mistakes/

Hassani, N. (2023, February 28). 31 types of succulents worth growing. The Spruce. https://www.thespruce.com/types-of-succulents-7090763

Hicks-Hamblin, K. (2021, September 29). The scientifically-backed benefits of companion planting. Gardener's Path. https://gardenerspath.com/how-to/organic/benefits-companion-planting/

Homegrown Garden. (n.d.). Which succulents can be planted together? Homegrown Garden. https://homegrown-garden.com/blogs/blog/which-succulents-can-be-planted-together

How to care for a Christmas Cactus: A complete guide. (2021, November 12). The Sill. https://www.thesill.com/blog/christmas-cactus

How to care for a Pencil Cactus plant. (n.d.). Greeneryunlimited.Co. https://greeneryunlimited.co/pages/pencil-cactus-care

How to grow a Christmas cactus. (n.d.). Miraclegro.com. https://miraclegro.com/en-us/indoor-gardening/how-to-grow-a-christmas-cactus.html

How to grow cacti & succulents. (n.d.). Horticulture Magazine. https://horticulture.co.uk/succulents/

How, G. K. (2016, April 9). Fertilizing cactus plants: When and how to fertilize A cactus. Gardening Know How. https://www.gardeningknowhow.com/ornamental/cacti-succulents/scgen/fertilizing-cactus-plants.htm

How, G. K. (2016, April 9). Fertilizing cactus plants: When and how to fertilize A cactus. Gardening Know How. https://www.gardeningknowhow.com/ornamental/cacti-succulents/scgen/fertilizing-cactus-plants.htm

Hughes, M. (2021, September 3). How to fix leggy plants for a lush indoor garden. Better Homes & Gardens. https://www.bhg.com/gardening/houseplants/care/fix-leggy-houseplants/

Iannotti, M. (2018, October 1). Crown of Thorns (Euphorbia milii): Care & Grow Guide. The Spruce. https://www.thespruce.com/crown-of-thorns-plant-4175182

Insect pests of cacti and succulents grown as house plants. (n.d.). Missouribotanicalgarden.org. https://www.missouribotanicalgarden.org/gardens-gardening/your-garden/help-for-the-home-gardener/advice-tips-resources/pests-and-problems/insects/mealybugs/insect-pests-of-cacti-and-succulents

Jade plant: How to grow and care for Jade plants – garden design. (2020, September 22). Gardendesign.com; Garden Design Magazine. https://www.gardendesign.com/succulents/jade-plant.html

Jagdish. (2021, May 10). Pruning in agriculture – benefits, tips, and ideas. Agri Farming. https://www.agrifarming.in/pruning-in-agriculture-benefits-tips-and-ideas

Jamie. (2021, September 3). How to fix leggy plants and seedlings + prevention tips. WhyFarmIt. https://whyfarmit.com/how-to-fix-leggy-plants/

Janie. (2020, October 5). Fertilizer for cactus: When, how and in what ratio. Succulent Alley. https://succulentalley.com/fertilizer-for-cactus/

Janie. (2020, September 29). How to plant cactus in ground: A step-by-step guide. Succulent Alley. https://succulentalley.com/how-to-plant-cactus-in-ground/

Janie. (2023, January 31). Can cactus and succulents be planted together? Succulent Alley. https://succulentalley.com/can-cactus-and-succulents-be-planted-together/

Johnson's Beehive Cactus (Echinomastus johnsonii). (n.d.). iNaturalist United Kingdom. https://uk.inaturalist.org/taxa/871500-Echinomastus-johnsonii

Lalko, A. (2023). Starfish Cactus: Plant Guide. Independently Published.

Limiterd, G. L. (n.d.). Ball cactus (Parodia magnifica) Flower, Leaf, Care, Uses – PictureThis. PictureThis. https://www.picturethisai.com/wiki/Parodia_magnifica.html

Mammillaria dixanthocentron. (n.d.). http://www.llifle.com/Encyclopedia/CACTI/Family/Cactaceae/19098/Mammillaria_dixanthocentron

McCarthy, K. (2018, July 3). Dividing succulents – propagating succulents. The Succulent Eclectic. https://thesucculenteclectic.com/dividing-succulents-propagating/

McKie, C. (2022). The Delicate Beauty of the Lady Finger Cactus. Houseplant Central. https://houseplantcentral.com/lady-finger-cactus/

McKie, C. (2022, September 20). The Starfish cactus: A unique beauty. Houseplant Central. https://houseplantcentral.com/starfish-cactus/

Mexican snow ball Care (Watering, Fertilize, Pruning, Propagation). (n.d.). PictureThis. https://www.picturethisai.com/care/Echeveria_elegans.html

Mexican Snowball plant care & growing basics: Water, light, soil, propagation etc. (n.d.). Myplantin.com. https://myplantin.com/plant/392

Miller, R. (2019, August 19). Where do most succulents come from? Succulent City; SucculentCity.com. https://succulentcity.com/where-do-most-succulents-come-from/

Miller, R. (2022, August 1). How to trim/ prune succulents successfully (an easy guide from A succulent expert). Succulent City; SucculentCity.com. https://succulentcity.com/how-to-trim-succulents/

Miller, R. (2022, August 7). 5 organic succulent fertilizers for naturally feeding your garden. Succulent City; SucculentCity.com. https://succulentcity.com/organic-succulent-fertilizer/

Miller, R. (2023). The Old Lady Cactus 'Mammillaria Hahniana' Succulent City. https://succulentcity.com/old-lady-cactus/

Old lady cactus Care (Watering, Fertilize, Pruning, Propagation). (n.d.). PictureThis. https://www.picturethisai.com/care/Mammillaria_hahniana.html

Old Lady cactus Plant Care & Growing Basics: Water, Light, Soil, Propagation, etc. (n.d.). Myplantin.com. https://myplantin.com/plant/393

Old man cactus Care (Watering, Fertilize, Pruning, Propagation). (n.d.). PictureThis. https://www.picturethisai.com/care/Cephalocereus_senilis.html

Old man cactus growing and plant care guide – good life vibez. (n.d.). Goodlifevibez.com. https://goodlifevibez.com/old-man-cactus-growing-and-plant-care-guide/

Old man cactus. (2016, January 5). Horticulture Unlimited. https://horticultureunlimited.com/plant-guide/old-man-cactus/

Opuntia microdasys bunny ears, angel's-wings PFAF plant database. (n.d.). Pfaf.org. https://pfaf.org/User/Plant.aspx?LatinName=Opuntia+microdasys

Oreocereus trollii old man of the mountain. (n.d.). Planet Desert. https://planetdesert.com/products/oreocereus-trollii-old-man-of-the-mountain-cactus-cacti-nice-real-live-plant

OREOCEREUS TROLLII. Old Man Of The Mountain Cactus. (n.d.). Thepalmtreecompany. https://www.thepalmtreecompany.com/product-page/oreocereus-trollii-old-man-of-the-mountain-cactus-1

Paschall, T. P. (2022, March 22). 5 ways to makeover an overgrown garden. Best Pick Reports. https://www.bestpickreports.com/blog/post/5-ways-to-makeover-an-overgrown-garden/

Pino, M. (2023, June 13). How to plant, grow, and care for queen of the Night Flower. Planet Natural. https://www.planetnatural.com/queen-of-the-night-flower/

Place, V. (2012). Page Not Found. Lulu.com. https://www.hgtv.com/outdoors/flowers-and-plants/how-to-plant-a-cactus-container-garden

Plant ID: Flowers and Foliage: Zebra Plant – Florida Master Gardener Volunteer Program – University of Florida, Institute of Food and Agricultural Sciences. (n.d.). https://gardeningsolutions.ifas.ufl.edu/mastergardener/outreach/plant_id/flowers_indoor/zebra_plant.html

PlantIn. (n.d.). Notocactus Magnificus Plant Care & Growing Basics: Water, Light, Soil, Propagation etc. | PlantIn. https://myplantin.com/plant/6212

Rahman, A. (2021, April 12). Signs of under-watered cactus (and how to revive it). Garden For Indoor.

Rana, A. (2023, February 10). Cactus care 101: Everything you need to know about having a cactus. Planet Desert. https://planetdesert.com/blogs/news/how-to-care-for-a-cactus

risk of overwatering of cacti and succulents – Google Search. (n.d.). Google.com.

https://www.google.com/search?q=risk+of+overwatering+of+cacti+and+succulen ts&oq=risk+of+overwatering+of+cacti+and+succulents&aqs=chrome..69i57.274 27j0j7&sourceid=chrome&i.e.,=UTF-8

risk of underwatering of cacti and succulent plants – Google Search. (n.d.). Google.com. https://www.google.com/search?q=risk+of+underwatering+of+cacti+and+succule nt+plants&oq=risk+of+underwatering+of+cacti+and+succulent+plants&aqs=chr ome..69i57j33i160l2.18649j0j7&sourceid=chrome&i.e.,=UTF-8

San Pedro column cactus Care (Watering, Fertilize, Pruning, Propagation). (n.d.-a). PictureThis. https://www.picturethisai.com/care/Echinopsis_pachanoi.html

San Pedro column cactus Care (Watering, Fertilize, Pruning, Propagation). (n.d.-b). PictureThis. https://www.picturethisai.com/care/Echinopsis_pachanoi.html

Sánchez, M. (2017, November 9). What are the parts of the cactus, and what functions do they have? Jardineria On. https://www.jardineriaon.com/en/partes-del-cactus-y-sus-funciones.html

Schiller, N. (2019, February 3). Propagating succulents in 5 easy steps. Gardener's Path. https://gardenerspath.com/how-to/propagation/succulents-five-easy-steps/

Schiller, N. (2022, July 7). How to grow succulents outdoors in the garden. Gardener's Path. https://gardenerspath.com/plants/succulents/grow-garden-succulents/

Sears, C. (2020, June 17). How to grow and care for chocolate soldier plant. The Spruce. https://www.thespruce.com/chocolate-soldier-plant-profile-5024790

Sears, C. (2021a, April 13). How to grow and care for Mexican snowballs. The Spruce. https://www.thespruce.com/mexican-snowballs-echeveria-elegans-profile-5120250

Sears, C. (2021b, June 30). How to grow and care for the bunny ear cactus. The Spruce. https://www.thespruce.com/bunny-ear-cactus-guide-5190802

Secuianu, M. (2020a, November 3). Old Lady Cactus guide: How to grow & care for "Mammillaria Hahniana." GardenBeast. https://gardenbeast.com/old-lady-cactus-guide/

Secuianu, M. (2020b, November 18). Brasiliopuntia Brasiliensis Guide: How to grow & care for "Brazilian Prickly Pear." GardenBeast. https://gardenbeast.com/brasiliopuntia-brasiliensis-guide/

Sher, S. (2021, September 30). 25 types of succulents that make great houseplants. Bob Vila; BobVila.com. https://www.bobvila.com/articles/types-of-succulents/

Spengler, T. (2018, February 24). Managing large shrubs – learn how to trim an overgrown shrub. Gardening Know How. https://www.gardeningknowhow.com/ornamental/shrubs/shgen/trimming-overgrown-shrub.htm

Staff, G. (2019, May 6). Austrocephalocereus dybowskii – Giromagi Cactus and Succulents. Giromagi Cactus and Succulents. https://www.giromagicactusandsucculents.com/austrocephalocereus-dybowskii-giromagi-cactus-succulents/

StaffSimone. (2022, May 30). Acanthocalycium thionanthum – Giromagi Cactus and Succulents. Giromagi Cactus and Succulents. https://www.giromagicactusandsucculents.com/acanthocalycium-thionanthum/

Stamp, E., & McLaughlin, K. (2018, September 12). How to care for succulents (and not kill them): 9 plant care tips. Architectural Digest. https://www.architecturaldigest.com/story/how-to-care-for-succulents

Stephens, T. (2019, May 29). A guide to watering cactus. Cactus Culture – Australia's Premium Online Cactus Shop. https://cactusculture.com.au/learning-centre/cactus-watering-guide

Stephens, T. (2022, August 29). Does a cactus need water? Cactus Culture – Australia's Premium Online Cactus Shop. https://cactusculture.com.au/learning-centre/does-a-cactus-need-water

Strawberry cactus care (watering, fertilizing, pruning, propagation). (n.d.-a). PictureThis. https://www.picturethisai.com/care/Mammillaria_dioica.html

Strawberry cactus care (watering, fertilizing, pruning, propagation). (n.d.-b). PictureThis. https://www.picturethisai.com/care/Mammillaria_dioica.html

Succulents Australia. (n.d.). Thimble Cactus – Mammillaria gracilis fragilis. https://www.succulents-australia-sales.com/products/thimble-cactus?variant=31372756222083

Taylor, L. H. (2016, June 30). 21 best cactus plants to grow in your garden. The Spruce. https://www.thespruce.com/best-cactus-to-plant-in-garden-4059807

Temperature and humidity. (2021, December 14). Plnts.com. https://plnts.com/en/care/doctor/temperature-and-humidity

The complete guide to trimming succulents. (n.d.). Lula's Garden. https://www.lulasgarden.com/blogs/all-blogs/the-complete-guide-to-trimming-succulents

The Ruth Bancroft Garden & Nursery. (2023, March 3). Echinopsis formosa – The Ruth Bancroft Garden & Nursery. https://www.ruthbancroftgarden.org/plants/echinopsis-formosa/

Tuttle, C. (2021, May 6). How to care for succulents indoors. Succulents and Sunshine. https://www.succulentsandsunshine.com/guide-growing-succulents-indoor-house-plants/

Ultimate guide: How to fight cactus diseases and pests. (2021, November 7). CactusWay. https://cactusway.com/ultimate-guide-how-to-fight-cactus-diseases-and-pests/

Vanderlinden, C. (2011, January 18). How to prevent leggy vegetable seedlings. The Spruce. https://www.thespruce.com/preventing-your-seedlings-from-getting-leggy-2539979

Vanderzeil, G. (2018, May 15). What's wrong with my succulent?! Collective Gen. https://collectivegen.com/2018/05/whats-wrong-succulent/

VanZile, J. (2008, October 23). How to grow and care for Kalanchoe. The Spruce. https://www.thespruce.com/growing-kalanchoe-plants-1902982

VanZile, J. (2008, September 11). How to grow and care for indoor cactus. The Spruce. https://www.thespruce.com/how-to-grow-cactus-1902954

VanZile, J. (2008, September 11). How to grow and care for indoor cactus. The Spruce. https://www.thespruce.com/how-to-grow-cactus-1902954

VanZile, J. (2009a, May 19). Ponytail Palm Plant Profile. The Spruce. https://www.thespruce.com/grow-beaucarnea-recurvata-1902886

VanZile, J. (2009b, November 17). How to care for Jade plants: Indoor growing guide. The Spruce. https://www.thespruce.com/grow-jade-plants-indoors-1902981

VanZile, J. (2022a). How to Grow and Care for Rat Tail Cactus. The Spruce. https://www.thespruce.com/aporocactus-flagelliformis-definition-1902538

VanZile, J. (2022b). How to Grow and Care for Ball Cactus. The Spruce. https://www.thespruce.com/grow-parodia-cacti-indoors-1902591

Waddington, E. (2023, May 17). 7 common cacti problems & solutions. Horticulture Magazine. https://horticulture.co.uk/cacti-problems/

west-coast-gardens. (2023, January 18). 5 care tips to keep your cactus happy. West Coast Gardens. https://www.westcoastgardens.ca/blogs/tips-inspiration/5-care-tips-to-keep-your-cactus-happy

Wet, & Forget. (2019, February 12). Fixes for the most common succulent pests and diseases. Life's Dirty. Clean Easy. https://askwetandforget.com/fixes-common-succulent-pests-diseases/

Weymouth, M. (2019, January 28). How to use rooting hormone when propagating plants. Martha Stewart. https://www.marthastewart.com/1535873/how-to-use-rooting-hormone

What is integrated pest management (IPM)? (n.d.). Ucanr.edu. https://ipm.ucanr.edu/what-is-ipm/

What is Pruning? Importance, Benefits & Methods of Pruning. (n.d.). Davey.com. https://blog.davey.com/what-is-pruning-the-importance-benefits-and-methods-of-pruning/

What is the best fertilizer for your cactus? (2021, February 23). CactusWay. https://cactusway.com/what-is-the-best-fertilizer-for-your-cactus/

White, J. (2022, June 23). 57 types of succulents with names and pictures. All About Gardening. https://www.allaboutgardening.com/types-of-succulents/

Why is Companion Planting So Important? (2023, June 19). Triangle Gardener Magazine; Triangle Gardener LLC. https://www.trianglegardener.com/why-is-companion-planting-so-important/

Wiley, D. (2015, June 9). How to grow cactus plants in cold-winter climates. Better Homes & Gardens. https://www.bhg.com/gardening/flowers/perennials/growing-cactus-plants-in-cold-climates/

Wolfe, D. (2020, June 3). The best pots for succulents of 2023. Bob Vila; BobVila.com. https://www.bobvila.com/articles/best-pots-for-succulents/

WoS. (2022). Epiphyllum hookeri (Hooker's Orchid Cactus). World of Succulents. https://worldofsucculents.com/epiphyllum-hookeri/

Yang, K. (2021, November 4). 5 surprising facts about cactus sustainability. Pricklee Cactus Water. https://pricklee.com/blogs/learn/cactus-sustainability

Young, C. (2023, May 8). The best tips on growing a San Pedro cactus. The Planted Pot. https://theplantedpot.co.nz/blogs/plant-care/san-pedro-cactus

Printed in the USA
CPSIA information can be obtained
at www.ICGtesting.com
LVHW042017310124
770343LV00002B/13

.